Merry-Go-Round

The Story of One Woman's Life

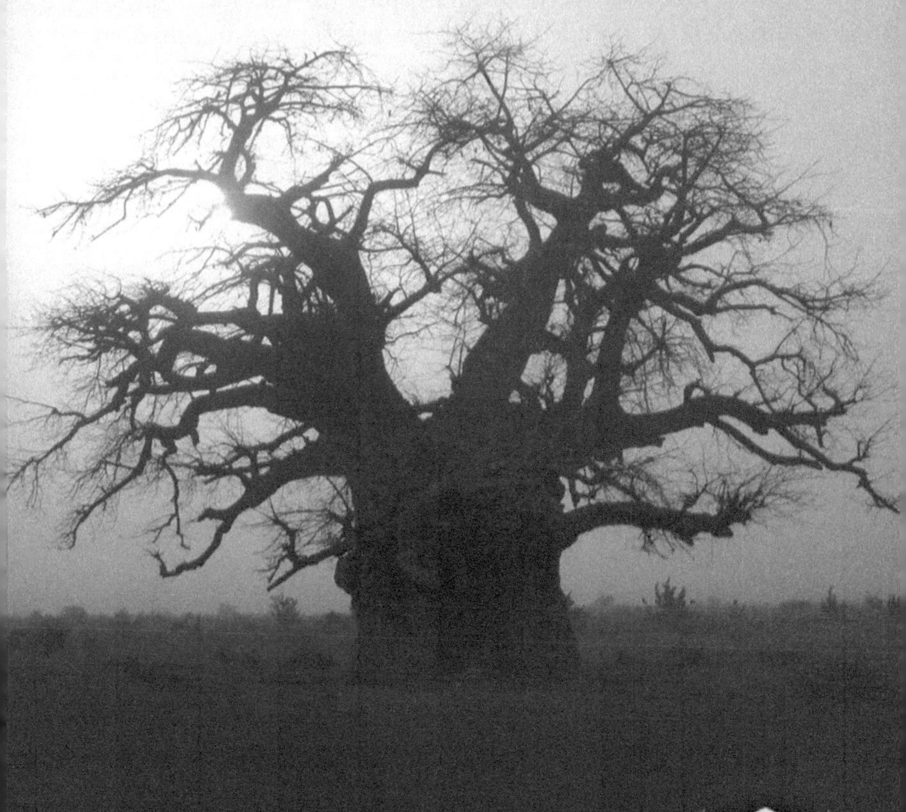

CAROL A. CRANDELL

WORKBOOK PRESS LLC
187 E Warm Springs Rd,
Suite B285, Las Vegas, NV 89119, USA

Website:https://workbookpress.com/
Hotline:1-888-818-4856
Email:admin@workbookpress.com

Ordering Information:
Quantity sales. Special discounts are available on quantity purchases by corporations, associations, and others.
For details, contact the publisher at the address above.

ISBN-13:   978-1-956876-99-4 (Paperback Version)

REV. DATE: 19/01/2022

Merry -Go- Round

The Story of One Woman's Life

Carol A. Crandell

For Deidre, Kerridwen, and Caitlin—
my legacy for the future;
and for Pat and Pete,
who believed in me.

Table of Contents

Prologue

Part I: Roots

A Poem You Might Have Written

Merry-Go-Round, go round and round,
From zenith to nadir and back again,
A ring of gold within my reach
But as it's worn, the green does stain.

Time repeats or so it seems,
A spiral never ending.
So where are we now, or are we here?
Which way were we wending?

A river valley all green and lush.
A sea coast with the sound of surf.
A desert highland covered with sage.
A forest of pine with needles as turf.

The doe and fawn, with a buck not far
Gaze on as I wander alone.
An eagle soars through clouded skies.
My cry to him, a soft low moan.

Yet with the dark there is yet hope
For a lighting is sure to be
And I know with truth that I'll carry through
Until the dawn of the day, I see.

I will rise with a hope that fills my heart.
For I know that I will endure.
And I'll find my way, through love and care.
Of this, I do know for sure.

Pete Serini
April 1, 2000

From Peter Serini, a longtime friend who wrote this after he read the unrevised version of Merry-Go-Round*. Thank you, Pete, for allowing me to use this.*

Prologue

Fragments of Our Lives

Between one of our many moves, the small, dome-top trunk stood half hidden in the shadows, behind a faded Victorian settee and beneath a stack of dusty hatboxes left in storage. I'd have to clear a path before I could drag it into the light. As I moved aside boxes of outgrown toys and delicate crystal, a childish anticipation arose within me, just like it always had when Mother lifted the lid of her keepsake trunk. Her grandfather had built the large three-by-five-foot trunk durable enough to withstand a train trip from Iowa to California and then to Oregon in the 1880s. A rope handle on each end gave handholds for anyone strong enough to use them. Mother had kept so many treasures in this trunk— the white Chinese silk, a delicately painted blue fan, and a silver child's ring, all brought home from the Far East by her brother Larry after World War II. She had kept her wedding dress here, Dad's yearbooks, and photographs...so many mementos. I had loved watching her reminisce over these things. But now a different trunk was filled with treasures that were mine, and I was looking for one in particular.

I paused to admire a floor lamp with an onyx base, then shoved aside the upright steamer trunk, and lifted the settee out of my way. Grasping the worn leather handles of the trunk, I tugged it away from the wall and raised the lid, a smile of anticipation on my face. The fragrance of cedar drove away the nose-tickling odor of dust. Tucked into the lid storage area, I found the black-and-white wool skunk Mother Marie had made for me, its once white fleece now dingy from the years it had sat on my bed. There, too, was the pink chenille dog, minus one eye—one of my first toys. My hands felt grimy from the dust, and I wiped them on the seat of my blue jeans. Carefully, I lifted aside my wedding dress, the white lace carefully packed in its plastic bag. Beneath that rested the tiny cap that Gerry had worn, along with Deidre's small turquoise wool poncho and her silver baby mug. I uncovered the Fenton plate that had come to me from Mother—originally a gift to her from old Mrs. Clark, a church friend in Mitchell, Oregon. When I held it to the light, the many hues of its iridescence shone as if ancient gems had been unearthed and brought into the sun. The marigold carnival glass, cheap in the 1920s, was rich, red-hued, and entrancing. Rewrapping it, I laid it aside. It was not what I sought.

At last, I found it—the Armand Marseille doll that had spent my childhood in Mother's trunk. There had been two other dolls—the blond china-head doll that had gone to Ruth, my middle sister, and the jointed composition doll without a head that my youngest sister Georgia should have gotten before it was destroyed by careless renters. But this one was mine. She had a bisque shoulder-plate head, composition forearms, and a kid body filled with sawdust. The open-shut eyes were loose inside the head, and the wig and pate had come unglued. The mohair wig was thin, combed too many times by little hands. The kid body remained intact, but the muslin lower legs needed additional sawdust and new stitching. I would need to reattach the arms correctly.

I turned the doll over, trying to imagine my grandmother as a girl. She must have been a careful child. The fragile bisque head showed no cracks or chips. The composition fingers were blunted with wear but intact. Even the tiny porcelain teeth in the open mouth were still in place. I sat back on my heels, wondering about the woman who had loved this doll.

From my research, I knew that Grandmother had been born in 1895, at Willamette Falls, Oregon. I have seen her grave and read her obituary. As a child, I'd wandered the rooms of the house she called home, but I did not know her because she died at age forty-one, six years before I was born. I lifted her wedding picture—still fresh behind its rounded glass within a gold frame—from its place beside the doll. I searched her face. I saw a pleasant woman wearing a slight smile. Next to her, Granddad looked stern—or do I think that because I know he never really liked having us children around? Looking at her again, I saw a large woman. Nothing fragile about her. She stood beside Granddad's chair looking taller than my five feet, two inches. She would have had capable hands and a comfortable lap on which to cuddle a child.

I shook my head. Would I ever understand the woman I had never known? I remembered prowling through her home as a child, admiring the dolls and the two bowls someone had stored in the upstairs window seat after she died, one cobalt, the other ruby-glazed. I had played her pump organ, balancing on the three-legged, claw-and-ball-footed oak stool. I had cranked the upright Victrola, sat on the slippery, black horsehair sofa, and spent hours pouring over the drawer full of black-and-white photos in the unused parlor. These were the sum of the unknown.

I can make assumptions by looking within myself. Grandmother loved beauty—the luster of glass, the warmth of rich woods. She played the organ and collected memories in the form of photos. She treasured the past, or I would not have her doll. She was a wife, a mother of two sons and a daughter. She managed a farmhouse and a farm complete with garden, orchard, cellar, and smokehouse. These traces of her presence reveal a woman of substance, but without her words in a diary or journal how can I know her thoughts, her hopes, or her dreams? To share my thoughts, my hopes, and my dreams, I write for those who follow me and for those, who like me, lived a less than perfect life. May my footprints act as a guide.

**

Circles

A choice is made,
A line is drawn—
A pebble falls
Spawning sun-bright
Ripples in still water.

The circles of my life,
Bright strands of moonlight
Twining, spiraling,
Forcing me to grow.

A spinning gyre,
My spirit climbs into the light,
Step by hesitant step
Until it pauses to reflect,
Retreat, reverse—

I descend
To walk the darker ways,
To seek out hurt and pain—
The demons of my past.
I pull their fangs—
I chase them out.

In strength I walk away.

Inner Landscape

I am Prussian blue
of hidden emotions
sparked
with red pinpoints of rage;

I am Chinese red
of creative energy
seeking, always,
an outlet;

I am black and white of well-ordered days
constrained,
making connections;

I am phosphorescent,
a haze
scintillating with imagination and dreams.

Part I
Roots

Chapter 1: My Beginning

I arrived in this world on July 8, 1942—six months after the Japanese bombed Pearl Harbor. I do not remember the war, but I do remember seeing ration cards in Mother's trunk. My personal connection to this time in history is a child's silver ring containing a red glass that looks like a ruby. My uncle Larry, Mother's youngest brother, sent it home for me while he was serving in the Pacific theater. I also remember that a few years later—it must have been shortly after the war—a neighbor living back in the mountains from us asked Dad to help him with the German displaced persons that he had accepted on his ranch. Dad's heritage was German, and he knew enough of the language to assist.

I was the eldest of three girls born to Clarence Herman and Edna Carol (Stephens) Schoenberger. They named me Carol Ann, Carol for "song," but why they chose Ann for my middle name, no one ever said. Ruth Minnie followed me on May 23, 1944, and Georgia Lee arrived July 30, 1947. Ruth carried the names of our grandmothers, and Georgia was the feminine for our paternal grandfather's name. At this time, we lived at Top, what the locals called the mountain and area behind it north of Monument, Oregon. Top, a basalt-capped mountain or butte overlooking Monument on one side and our home on the backside, was ever-present in my young life. The flat plateau of the mountaintop was home to a lookout tower that I could see whenever I looked up.

I am the fourth generation from George G. Schoenberger, the German immigrant who came from Germany in 1857 with his Irish wife, Bridget, two sons, Peter and John, and a daughter, Christena. George G. was naturalized in 1870 in Wisconsin, but the only early information coming down to us is from his application. It states the date of his immigration and his arrival in the port at New York City. My cousin and I have searched but not been able to move back from that point—too many records were lost during the war.

We learned that one child was born near Essen and another near Berlin, but that has never helped. There seems to have been a family reticence about personal history. I do know that the first generation spoke German in the home. A few pictures came down to me after my Aunt Dora's death in the 1960s. I used one of George G. with a cigar stuck in his mouth as the cover picture for the family notebook that I built to give my half-sister some idea of the family she did not know. Born from Dad's first marriage, Margaret is older than I am. We have connected, but too many years apart have not made us close. She grew up without Daddy. Between her mother and mine, her letters never reached Dad, and if he wrote, she never received his letters.

Dad's father, George Nicholas, born in Wisconsin, married Minnie Augusta Bramer, and they raised their family in Beaver Dam, Wisconsin. Dad told few if any stories of his youth. I do remember that he mentioned the cold and snowy winters, one in particular when the snow was deep enough to hide the fences.

Mother's families were early settlers in Oregon. At only six months old, her father came to Oregon on one of the first trains to the west. His family settled in the Heppner wheat country. Virgil Stephens, my great-grandfather, raised horses at the time of World War I and sold stock to the military. I have traced the Stephenses back to Iowa and Kentucky, and after many years of searching, put together the clues that led to Virginia and beyond. Ruth Rue Stephens, my grandmother, also came of pioneer stock. The Rues and Scotts traveled to Oregon with a wagon train. That is how my grandfather Joseph Rue met my grandmother Lula Scott.

Isaac Scott, Lula's father, is buried in a cemetery in La Grande. Some time after his death, his wife Susan (Cumpston) Scott moved to the Willamette Valley. I traced the Scotts to their immigrant ancestor who arrived in Georgia from Scotland. The Rues came from Illinois but originated in the areas of New York and New Jersey. Some of the connections are vague, but most likely they were Huguenots coming from France.

Mother's lineage branched back to the Tibbetts and then to the Ridlons of Maine and the Orkney Isles. Tracing those families for Daughters of the American Revolution (DAR) and Daughters of American

Colonists (DAC) gave me practical experience in family research. With that data as a base, I continued my searching, with help from Aunt Alice and Aunt Lavinia, wives of Mother's brothers. We traced to the Dungan and Latham families of England, and then continued back into history.

As my eighth-grade teacher said, I am a "duke's mixture"—someone with no single nationality prevailing. The German reticence and forbearance came down to me, as did the tendency to heart disease. On the other hand, from Mother I received a face that hasn't wrinkled as I grow older, and hair that is thin and greyed early. On the downside, the gene for alcoholism also came from Mother through her Stephens' blood. I also received the hidden talents of "knowing" and healing from her. As a teacher, I seemed to have eyes in the back of my head. The kids never understood how I always knew when they were off-task or up to something other than schoolwork.

**

The Early Years

Childhood

There was blue-patterned linoleum
and a brown metal floor grate,
warmth from rising heat,
voices, often low—sometimes raised,
a sidewalk bordered with flowers,
a millpond, fascinating, but forbidden.

Then I remember a ranch house
with grey-brown boards
rain-streaked with age.

There were kittens to cuddle
a tom to beware of—
school where kittens were taught
to romp and play in a roll of wire fencing.

There were nights with Daddy
under the stars,
a split-rail fence with splinters—
the grandeur of falling stars
against a black velvet sky.

There was Shep, a puppy,
grey, black, and white—
a jealous guard
watching over small charges.

I remember the dirt road—
adventure in splashy puddles,

spring freshets,
snowdrifts—an unbroken
expanse to autograph.

There were spring flowers,
summer roses,
the yeasty odor of newly
harvested wheat, and
the cutting edges of new stubble.
I remember the hot resin odor
from pines oozing pitch
in late July,
the sour bite of ripe chokecherries, and
the crisp crunch of a new carrot
fresh pulled from the garden.

There was spring water, icy
against my teeth, and
Watercress, peppery
on my tongue.

I remember summer days with
blue skies inhabited by
fleecy dragons and ships
and castles…
green grass, soft to my bare feet, and
black mud that squished
between my toes.

There was the lazy drone of honeybees and
a rustling of leaves
high in the cottonwoods;
the acrid odor
of bright nasturtiums
as I brushed past
along the terrace path.

I remember the softness, the warmth of
Blackie and White Paw
snuggled tight against me
on a cold and snowy night...
the raccoon rug, nestling
bare toes before a wood fire...
the velvet flank of Babe, the Jersey cow, and
warm milk, fresh from the pail,
steam from her breath hanging
in the chill fall air.

I remember chaff and dust motes,
the dusty closeness
within the dim barn
the peacefulness of animals...
Home.

Life on the Ranch at Top

Living at Top was paradise for children, although we did not realize it at the time. It wasn't large as ranches go, yet as children, we never found its limits. Twelve hundred acres of timber on steep slopes with only forty acres of tillable ground was too small for raising cattle. Dad ran twenty head of beef stock besides Babe, the family milk cow. He never had a bull or horse. I looked forward to the day that he would decide a horse was necessary, but he never did. Horses ate too much, and the neighbor's bulls always managed to show up when needed.

As children, Mother allowed us to run wild as long as we told her where we were going and then returned when she called. We roamed through the pine-timbered slopes playing our version of the Lone Ranger and Tonto, jumping sagebrush with never a thought about snakes. I never saw a rattler, but we felt safe with our "guns" (pointed fingers, as Mother had forbidden toy guns or sticks that could hurt us if we fell on them). Through the spring and summer, we would pick wildflowers—pale pink sweet peas, scarlet Indian paintbrush, sunflowers, purple lupine, fuzzy kitten's britches, and anything else we thought was pretty or smelled nice.

The creek that ran through the ranch became a favorite haunt. Sometimes in the hot summer, we'd tuck our skirts up into our panties—no shorts or swimsuits for us—and then in the shade of overhanging brush and willows, we'd splash and play. Often there was as much mud as water. Ground springs created a boggy stretch along the creek where it ran downhill through the pastures. As the cows grazed, their feet raised hummocks and punched holes in the soft earth. We would hop from one dry spot to another to traverse this area.

We had one much-loved spot that could only be reached by crossing the pasture where Babe, the Jersey cow, liked to spend her afternoons. We would wait until she was at a distant corner, and then we'd sneak through the strands of barbed wire and run like mad for the opposite fence. If she spotted us, she would charge with her head lowered. She hated children!

Eventually the creek dropped over a ledge to form a waterfall. As a child, I thought it was enormous and beautiful. Cool spray misted the air under tall pines that shaded the creek side. Ruth and I clambered the steep slopes like two kid goats. As a mother, I wonder how my mother ever survived. Had she seen us, I am certain she would have switched our backsides. But, oh the fun!

The barn was a playground. Ruth and I wanted to fly, so we would clamber from the fence to the roof of the calf shed and jump off. Then we tried the barn rafters that were higher still, but we could swing from them to land on the mountain of chopped hay, sliding clear to the bottom or finding ourselves buried in a slide of hay. Dad really laid into us for that escapade, as we were playing there while the chopper was still filling the barn.

In the winter, there were snowy slopes on which to slide, using any available slick material or even a plain sled. The unmarked snow cried for angels or snowmen and snow fights. In cold winter weather, we delighted in tucking our bare toes into the coonskin rugs beside the heating stove. Mom had tanned the skins and then sewn two or three together, depending on their size, to make rugs. Even though, we used these rugs until our toes felt spots with no fur and holes, they never lost their odor that was rather like salty, old meat—a smokehouse sort of smell.

Summers were always hot. Dad put the forty acres into wheat and a field of alfalfa. The alfalfa and the pastures always needed water, and the wheat turned golden as it ripened. Harvest arrived in July, always a bummer for me. I don't think I ever had a birthday party because everyone was involved with harvest—combining the wheat and trucking it to storage.

Ruth and I spent our hours playing house, climbing the cherry tree or the wild chokecherry trees, pulling legs off grasshoppers or impaling them on porcupine quills to make them spit tobacco juice. We made mud pies decorated with catkins from the cottonwood trees.

Sometimes we simply lay on the grass and watched the clouds sail overhead. We conjured fantasies of ships and dragons.

Mother always had a large garden, planted where the original horse barn had stood. She loved working in it, but I hated getting my hands in the dirt. As a result, I did most of the housework and cooking. I did have to do my share in the potato patch, however. Dad did not spray for insects; therefore, Ruth and I handpicked the potato bugs and beetles that thrived on the green potato leaves. We also helped harvest the vegetables that Mother canned to feed us year round.

Store-bought groceries were rare. I cannot even remember what Mother bought except for the staples of salt, sugar, flour, and spices. A bag of red-and-white striped mints or cookies was a rare treat. Mother baked the bread we ate, canned our fruits and vegetables, and made cottage cheese and butter from the cow's milk. Our meat came from a calf or pig that we raised. Chickens provided us with eggs, meat, and even feathers for pillows.

To get from the ranch at Top to Grandpa's, Daddy always went across Sunflower Flat, unless we had been to church in Spray first. We passed Mrs. Scott's home, a "rich guy's place" on the right, and then the Van Dusen place. After that came Sunflower Flat, the sawmill, and finally the paved highway to Hardman where Uncle John and his daughter Alta Stevens lived. On one visit, Alta gave each of us girls a glass container filled with candy. Mine was a car painted red on the inside. Ruth's was an ocean steamer. Whenever we went through Hardman, almost a ghost town then, Mom would always point out the house where Ruth had been born. It was empty, weathered grey, and not much of a house.

Dad got our dog Shep, an Australian shepherd/collie mix, from Lyle Van Dusen when Georgia was six months old. When Lyle was a young man, and I was five, I intended to marry him when I grew up. Instead, when I was in the eighth grade, I spent a week helping out after his first baby was born. I was ahead with my schoolwork so was permitted to skip a week of school because he and his new wife needed someone to help around the house. I was there to help with cooking and cleaning, and Lyle would call me between five and six in the morning to make breakfast. I do not recall her name, but the image that stands out for me from that time is one of a red-haired woman with head bent over a nursing infant. As that was my first exposure to a newborn and nursing, I was embarrassed yet fascinated. I wanted to watch her but was ashamed to be seen looking.

Later, when I was in high school and they had at least two children, Lyle's wife was driving along the river road and ran head on into a logging truck. As I heard it, the log-truck driver honked and honked, but she ignored him. Two tiny children in the rear seat survived, but she was decapitated. What happens to our dreams?

Chapter 2: Parents

Daddy

You were the standard
I measured against
As you made me search out answers,
When you tossed the bales high,
Or told me to try again
As I let the tractor die.
If only
I could turn back the years
To sit and talk
Not father to daughter
But woman to man.

My Father

I guess kids cannot really "see" their parents. Looking back, I have no clear mental images of them at all. They were simply there, and I was secure in that knowledge. Dad was much quieter than Mother. He had a slow but subtle humor, and I had to learn when he was teasing. His dark brown eyes would give him away if I watched them closely. They always twinkled when he was enjoying himself. At five feet, seven inches, he was not a tall man although he loomed large in my life. He kept his weight between 160 and 180 pounds and seemed as solid and permanent as a mountain. He never tanned to the usual golden brown in the summer; instead, his face and bare arms burned red, almost mahogany from his work in the sun. As a young man, his hair was black, but by the time he turned fifty, it was raddled with grey. At seventy-six, it was iron grey, not white. His brown eyes were set wide in a strong face with broad cheekbones and a wide mouth that smiled easily. He was always clean-shaven.

Dad was of sturdy farmer stock—solidly built but not squatty. His size 8E feet were slightly pigeon-toed. His hands were those of a worker, strong, broad with stubby fingers, and palms like leather from calluses. When he was not teaching, he preferred to wear striped bib overalls with numerous pockets for all sorts of things.

Although Dad was an excellent teacher who gave more than twenty years, some of those before he married Mother, to the students of Oregon, he was always happier to be tearing down an engine for repair or riding a tractor in the hayfield. He had a special way with animals too. The cows knew his touch. They would tolerate me at milking time until he arrived, but then they would bawl a welcome to him and cease to do anything at all for me. Even Shep, who always had to be with us girls, was Dad's dog at heart, and when he was eventually fatally injured, he refused to die until Dad got home.

Back then, the life of a rural teacher was hard. In 1948 and 1950 when he taught at Spray, Oregon, Dad had to provide his own housing—a canvas tent-house set on a wooden floor. Heat came from an oil stove that had a five-gallon reservoir that Dad had to refill each evening. Mother cooked our meals on her three-burner kerosene stove and baked in a portable oven placed over a burner. A chamber pot and an outhouse provided toilet facilities. Inadequate pay for teachers meant summer work on the ranch to provide food for the winter. When he retired in 1963, his final salary was $5,300 for the school year.

As a girl, I generally respected and admired my father. I would not say I was close to him, although there were times we seemed to have an unspoken rapport, especially as I reached my later teens. As a child, if I really wanted permission to do something, I would often go to Daddy because Mother might say no.

One Christmas, Ruth and I wanted to bring in the Christmas tree. We were still living at Top, and there must have been twelve to fourteen inches of snow on the level at the time. Dad let us go with a handsaw to cut our tree. We headed for the timber above the house and could find nothing to suit us. We circled the entire place, winding up on the edge of the south wheat field before we found our tree. There were few trees left to choose from, but we finally settled on a juniper with a trunk at least four inches through. And then we took only the top. Dad could not have been too happy about that.

As we trudged back home across the white, snow-covered field hours later, it was all we could do to drag our prize. We reported in to Daddy, who was still in his shop, and then answered Mother's frantic berating with, "Daddy knew where we were." He had kept our secret, and I imagine she must have worried over us for several hours. At any rate, the house smelled of juniper, not fir that year.

I think Daddy understood more of our growing pains than we gave him credit for. Mother was quite strict with Ruth and me. I was a senior in high school before Mother cut my hair to just above the shoulders and with bangs. Ruth begged until Mother, from sheer frustration, cut hers first. We did not wear shorts, and

I didn't own a pair of jeans or slacks. Facial makeup was unheard of at home. Overall, that made me the ideal candidate for a home economics demonstration on evening makeup. The class was the last period of the day, and I had no time to clean it off my face before going directly to my clerical work at the Rural Electric Association (REA) office. I really did not want to scrub it off yet, either.

Dad's Willys station wagon was in need of repairs, so he came for me in a Model A that Bud Crandell had left there when he entered the air force. Of course, Dad really enjoyed the car too. When I got into the car beside him, he looked me over well and without a word gave me an admiring look that said more than any words could have. He was proud to be seen with me. His look was that of a man eying a good-looking woman—recognition of me, not just his daughter. Nothing Mother said could dampen that memory, although a good scrubbing was an immediate must as soon as I got home. I saw Dad look that way one other time—as he lifted Georgia's wedding veil from her face and gave her to Gene. He really loved us in his quiet, caring way.

Mama

Permit me to tell you about Mama,
who hid her insecurity
behind big words and Bible verses.

She raised three children,
planted and harvested an enormous
garden each year,
and still found time to read.

But the Mama I remember most
taught WRONG with a willow switch,
rocked the upset child,
comforted with a hug,
and, to this very day
wants to be needed.

My Mother

Mothers are rarely appreciated until their daughters grow up and become mothers themselves. Then, I think, a bond of kinship is closer than the blood tie. Mothers are too busy rearing their children to do all the things that make someone stand out in a child's memory. That was the way it was with Mother.

She was a small person when I was young. When Georgia was an infant, Mom must have weighed ninety pounds. As a sophomore, I tried on a suit that she had worn, and it fit me. A year later, at 105 pounds, I was too big to fasten the skirt—and my waist measured a mere twenty-four inches at the time. Mother had blue eyes, and she wore her brown hair rolled away from her face or pulled back into a bun. She always wore gold, wire-framed glasses. Her hair began to grey when she was in her thirties, and by age fifty-five, she was nearly white. I inherited this genetic trait. I began greying in my twenties and by forty had very little brown left. Mom's nose was straight and rather thin, a smaller version of her father's Stephens nose. Her mouth set easily into a thin line. I don't remember her as a lighthearted person, but always as someone serious.

When we girls were sick, she nursed and cuddled us. When we were naughty, she spanked us. She taught us early how to do for ourselves and to help her. I learned to sew, first with a needle and only then with her sewing machine—a Singer featherweight electric that Dad had modified for her by improvising a handle that she could turn to run the machine without electricity. She taught me to cook simple foods and to can. I was in 4-H, yet Mother taught me most of what I learned.

She also gave me lessons in ironing—a most hated job. The woodstove in the basement heated the sadirons well, but it also heated me. Mother had three irons and one handle. I would place the irons on the stovetop to heat and then insert the handle, held by a potholder, into the hot iron. Holding it in my right hand, I would run the iron across the fabric lying on the ironing board that was padded with an old flannel blanket and covered by a sheet discolored from repeated ironings. Because these irons did not hold water to form steam, every piece of fabric had to be sprinkled with water, rolled, and placed into the ironing basket before I could iron. Cotton fabric often retained wrinkles that were hard to remove. I would wet my hand in a pan of water and sprinkle the wrinkles again before pressing with the hot iron. When an iron cooled, I would set it back on the range, place the handle in a fresh iron, and repeat the process. Thus, I learned.

Mother found it important that I play the piano, and she taught me to read music when I was big enough to sit at the keyboard. Mr. Akers, the music teacher one year at Monument, gave me several lessons on "Whispering Hope."

As we grew up, so did Mother. I really think she learned from us, although she often fought new or changing ideas. She tried very hard to live by the values and guidelines instilled in her by Grandma Lula (Scott) Rue, who mothered her following the death of her own mother Ruth Stephens in 1936. To say the least, Mother's values were Victorian in character. For instance, ladies crossed their ankles, not their legs; they wore hats or sunbonnets to keep the sun from tanning their faces. They did not swear. And a girl was an old maid by eighteen. Mother was a very modest person. She was also fanatically religious. What she believed, she tried to inculcate in us children. There was never a grey area for Mother. Something was either black or white, or right or wrong. She took her Bible teaching in a literal sense and taught us to do likewise. Mother held little room in her mind for any interpretation other than that handed down by the fire-and-brimstone preachers who were the source of spiritual edification in our lives in the late 1940s and 1950s. Men like Brother Samples, Brother Heard, and my future father-in-law, Frank Frederick Crandell, delineated the path we were to walk.

It was hard to live by my mother's precepts; rules that forbade haircuts, makeup, movies, and dances. In a small community, a school dance or a movie was about the only excuse for a boy to ask a girl for a date. I think Mother felt insecure and had rather low self-esteem. She never knew just what she was capable of doing until she had to take hold of the managerial reins when Dad's health began to fail following a stroke and the onset of Parkinson's disease in the midsixties.

When Dad began to fail, Ruth and I were both married; only Georgia remained at home. I think she benefited from Mother's experience with Ruth and me. Mom was much more liberal in her attitude toward Georgia's dress, hair, and makeup. Too, there was only one girl left at home, and financially the folks were doing better. They had more money to do the things Georgia wanted. Her wardrobe when she graduated from high school contained more items than I had owned the whole time I was home.

In many ways, Mother was too trusting of us, and I am sure we took advantage of her. Although she had strictly warned us girls about boys and their wandering hands, she permitted unchaperoned excursions, which could—and did—eventually create problems. Ruth ran away from high school with Nick, who became her first husband. Overall, however, Mother trusted us. I know that this acted as a restraint for me. My behavior was in my control because she trusted me to do right. When I transgressed her teaching and did not tell her that a foursome was reduced to three—my date for the movie, the other guy, and me—I did so knowingly and suffered mental recriminations and a heavy burden of guilt. Even now, sometimes, it is difficult not to feel guilty if I act contrary to her teaching, although as a woman I have made my own choices and determined my own code of behavior.

To see Mother at her best, one must see her with her grandchildren. She mothered all of them as much as she could, but with Sandra, Ron, and Deidre, she had a hand in shaping their lives. Because of marital problems, Ruth was at home off and on during her first years of marriage. In fact, she was home during most of her pregnancy with Sandra after Nick abandoned her in California, and Mother took her to Prineville where Ron was born. I was staying with Mom when Deidre was born. Bud and I were living in a mobile home in the Beaverton area at that time, but I wanted my child to be born under Dr. Rose's care in La Grande, just as Gerry, her brother, had been. When I returned to work nine months later, we were again living in Union. Mother babysat for Didi during the day while I worked.

Chapter 3: Grandparents

I remember…
the smell of cinnamon and allspice
wood smoke
the locust blooming in spring
at Grandpa Stephens's.

If we exist only as others remember us, my grandparents still exist. Grandpa Stephens and Mother Marie were my only grandparents still living when I was small, and they are a part of my early memories. If I close my eyes, I can still see Grandpa, tall with a shock of white hair parted on the left and falling in a cowlick across his forehead. His mustache was yellowed from both strong tea and the tobacco that he chewed. I see him in a white shirt with suspenders to hold up his trousers. He was someone to be wary of as he didn't really like little children. He was gruff, but I do not recall him ever laying a hand on any of us. Besides that, he allowed us children the run of the ranch when we visited, and he gave us his empty beer bottles to cash in. We gleaned at least one case each time we visited. On the way home to Top, Daddy would stop at the general store/76 gas station in Hardman where we could exchange the bottles for goodies.

Because he was old when I was young, he no longer actively farmed or ranched the property. Grandpa was just there, sometimes with old Sailor, the black-and-white cow dog with matted hair and strong doggy odor. Sometimes Grandpa was ensconced in his favorite oak chair, straight-backed with wire twisted between its legs for stability. He'd sit with the chair tipped back on two legs so that he could rest his feet on either the round oak table or the fender of the cook stove. For a little girl, his propped-up legs were an insurmountable barrier. He'd say, "Crawl under!" and crawl, I would. It was either that, remain cornered, or go outside through the kitchen and return through the seldom-used formal front door, or the reverse—go out the front to return through the back porch and kitchen.

The memories I hold are those of a child visiting a familiar place. I began life there, but by the time I was five, we lived on the ranch at Top, across the mountains from the Hardman-Heppner wheat country. It was the wheat that had brought my father to Grandpa's ranch in the first place. Daddy needed work, and there was wheat to harvest. He and Mother married on December 24, 1940, and began their life together there on Grandpa's ranch.

Even though Mother talked about Grandma Rue and Aunt Britta Strom, they were people who lived somewhere far away. Pictures in mother's photo album put a face to Grandma Rue, and Aunt Britta dressed a small doll in crocheted dress and hat for each of us girls. For me, Grandma was Mother Marie, Grandpa's second wife, a mail-order bride who came from Canada in 1947. She was a short woman, comfortably rounded in all the best places. She had rather frizzy white hair, gold-rimmed glasses, and always wore print-fabric bibbed aprons. She stayed up late at night working jigsaw puzzles and smoking cigarettes. I remember doing dishes at her house and being told that the way I wrung out the dishcloth showed I had strong hands. She told me she had never seen a dishcloth so dry. That made me very proud. Even today, I carefully wring out all the excess moisture before I wipe the table or the counters.

One year for Christmas when I was seven, Ruth was five, and Georgia was three, Grandma made clown dolls for Ruth and Georgia and a black-and-white skunk for me. She had taken requests during the summer so that she could give us something we wanted. That skunk remained as one of two mementos from my early childhood until someone broke into our storage shed and stole my dome-top trunk in 1995.

The summer I was ten, I spent several weeks with Grandma while Grandpa was in the hospital with yellow jaundice. I do not think I had ever been away from home before. Although I really wanted to stay with Grandma, I felt lost as I watched Dad's Jeep drive away. I remember going into the darkened parlor where

I curled up on the stuffed horsehair settee and cried. The first two nights were bad. I did not have nightmares, but my mind played tricks on me before I fell asleep. When I closed my eyes, I would see gigantic clipboards and enormous balls and shapes of foam rubber closing in on me. These spells recur even now as an adult when I am under extreme stress. I feel totally helpless and unable to escape. This was terrifying to me as a child because I found it very difficult to explain what was wrong.

Of an evening, Grandma and her daughter Edna, who had come to visit from Edmonton, Alberta, would sit up late putting together picture puzzles. I stayed up with them until I almost fell asleep over the puzzle. That began my night-owl habit. As Grandma searched the puzzle pieces, an unending chain of cigarettes would pass between her fingers. Beside her on one corner of the table stood a bottle whose contents were clear like water, and I remember Grandma saying, "I drink it to keep Grandpa from drinking it because it makes him sick." Being a gullible child, I believed her.

That summer I learned that skunks could be pets as well as wild animals. Grandma had one that had the run of a small bedroom off the parlor. Even with the scent gland removed, he had an unpleasant odor because she kept him captive indoors. The room, even when cleaned, always smelled of urine and feces. I suppose kitty litter was yet to be invented. I did not really like him, as he would bite my fingers. Along with the skunk, Grandma also had a Pekinese dog, the first of that kind that I had seen. I thought he looked funny with his nose smashed flat into his face.

Edna drove us to Heppner twice a week to visit Grandpa. While we were there, Grandma would visit a friend who lived in an upstairs apartment near, if I remember correctly, Doc Tibble's office. These days were hot, and I remember the locust trees because they provided nice shade.

On one of the trips to Heppner to visit Grandpa, Grandma allowed me to shop at the five-and-ten store. I wanted real furniture for my dollhouse but had a difficult time choosing from the assortment on display. Finally, I selected four pieces that cost a grand sum of forty cents. I chose a dark mahogany china hutch and a three-piece bedroom ensemble that looked like blond oak. Of course, the pieces were plastic, but they were sturdy. The only casualty in years of playing was the bed—the headboard broke loose from the rails, but I mended it with glue. These treasured items went into the dollhouse, fashioned from a four-compartment baby chick box that Ruth and I used for paper dolls.

I became interested in Grandma's steel guitar that summer. I must say, she tried to teach me. Given enough time, I might have learned to play because I liked the steel and pick instead of bare fingers, but time ran too quickly, and the summer was soon gone. Besides the guitar, I discovered pulp westerns, written as serials and full of romance and adventure. I do not know who read them first, but I found them stored in Uncle Art's room. I consumed each of them from cover to cover.

Grandma sewed dresses for me, bought doll furniture, made me a skunk, gave me chores, and praised me for wringing the dishrag dry. Although I did not know her well, she filled a need in my heart. She was warm yet mysterious—a woman who cared enough to enfold me in her circle of love and laughter and to feed my yearnings for new adventure and beauty. She loved me.

The Stephens Ranch

Memories of childhood visits all run together to form a composite picture of Grandpa's ranch. The narrow dirt road leading from the highway crossed a cattle guard and wound between wheat fields before crossing the creek on a wooden bridge. In the spring, the serviceberry bushes overhung the bridge and shed their creamy blossoms in our path. By late summer, we'd enjoy purple-black berries waiting to be picked. The road ended at the yard fence, where an old-fashioned yellow rose grew beside the gate. In summer, the small, fragrant, butter-yellow blooms cascaded on both sides of the fence, and behind that was the weathered frame farmhouse.

Through the gate, the sidewalk crossed a yard bordered with tall locust trees that flowered each spring, perfuming the air with their sweet, almost cloying fragrance. The grass grew unwatered for the most part except along the back porch. In spring, the purple grape hyacinths thrust their spears of color above the unmown grass. In summer, the hollyhocks along the fence provided us toys—globes tightly filled with seeds, and flute-shaped blossoms of pink, white, and red. Below them in the grass, we found malva weed with tiny flowers and small green seedpods that crunched between our teeth, providing a free, nutty-tasting snack. We entered the house through the back porch and kitchen. The formal entry with porch and parlor faced the hill away from the highway, because the original road up the valley had followed that side of the creek until the state built a much straighter, paved road up the other side.

The outdoors was a different yet familiar world for two little girls who came to visit its delights. Used to exploring mountain slopes where pine trees captured the wind in their tops, we found the creek bottom where Grandpa's place sprawled, dusty yet intriguing. Weeds grew tall, providing a jungle to explore in a backyard that had gone wild. They overgrew the garden, but horseradish plants and gooseberry bushes remained. As a child, I sampled the gooseberries right off the plant! Behind the backyard and the garden, a narrow footbridge crossed the creek, giving access to the orchard. At one time, this orchard must have been the pride of the valley. In the fall, Winesaps, Gravensteins, and other apples littered the ground where pigs had once dined. The farrowing huts—small triangular structures—provided perfect playhouses. They even came equipped with seats—planks that ran along each side to keep the sow from squashing her piglets. Grandpa must have raised lots of pigs at one time, and many of these A-frame huts remained in the orchard. Though dusty, these houses provided hours of play for little girls.

The old barn and corrals remained. The horses were long gone, but a few saddles with dry, cracking leather were there, cast aside in a corner. Mourning doves and swallows lived high in the rafters, and bright shafts of sunshine full of golden dust motes showed where shingles were missing. There were still traces of hay in the loft, but old, rusted machinery parts lay forgotten in the stalls, and dried dung and dust covered the floor.

Abandoned near the barn was an old car. No doubt sporty in its time, it was a two-door convertible without a top. The wheels had wooden spokes and the controls on or near the steering wheel actually worked. Ruth and I had many adventures in that old vehicle.

The barn was not the only building to explore. The blacksmith shop had odd, rusted pieces of metal lying around and windows made of stacked bottles. Ruth and I often sat in the old bunkhouse, recalling Zane Grey and his stories of the West. The smokehouse was still there, empty except for jars and other oddities; its dusty, tinny odor hinted of smoke and meat cure. Saved for the last, I remember the root cellar with its dark coolness and ever-present cobwebs. It was underground beneath the smokehouse and always dark and damp—an endless source of fear and fascination. Ruth and I would creep down the cobwebby steps beneath a creaky, wooden door that we just knew would close at any moment. Once down, we'd find only sprouting potatoes and empty jars on dusty shelves. No harmless garter snake ever spooked us, although we always expected one. Ruth and I revisited these intriguing places each time we went to Grandpa's.

Then there was the house itself. The upstairs was always hot—I must have gone up there only in the summer. There were two rooms with a small landing and hallway between. A window seat looked over the dried-up lawn and out to the burned brown hills. The stairs were narrow and steep; at the bottom was a formal foyer where an old pump organ stood that Grandma allowed me to play, although my music must have been noise to adult ears. I still remember how much work it took to pump enough air into the bellows to create sound when I pressed the keys. That foyer had been designed as a front hall, yet the house was situated so that everyone now came through the back porch and kitchen.

As you stood in the foyer, Grandpa's bedroom, separate from Grandma's, was on the right and the parlor with a bay window on the left. A closed porch ran across the front of the house, with part of it turned into a bedroom where the skunk lived. In the parlor, an upright Victrola stood beside a rocking chair, opposite a Victorian settee and a four-legged lamp table. The base of the Victrola held a drawer filled with old family photos. They are all gone now, burned in the ranch fire about 1951. I have often wondered how many ancestors that I know only as names on a pedigree chart were represented in those snapshots.

A huge kitchen, the heart of this house where everyone

gathered, was just off the parlor. Grandma cooked on a large, wood burning range with a warming oven and chrome trim that she kept polished to a gleam. The hub of the room, a forty-eight-inch round oak table, reigned beneath the large window. This table sat on a ten-inch-round pedestal with four clawed feet. When our family visited, we made it larger by inserting two twelve-inch leaves. At this table, each family member claimed a specific chair, and little girls definitely did not want to sit in the wrong chair. In addition, special spoons, one for Grandpa and one for Uncle Art, stood in a silver spooner that sat beside the sugar bowl in the center of the table. Little girls did not use those either.

To one side of the kitchen was a two-room addition with sloping ceilings and step-down floors. The pantry contained a Kitchen Queen cabinet with two large bins for flour and sugar. Above the working surface where Grandma rolled pie crusts or cut biscuits, stood closed storage that held a flour sifter and spices. The odor of cinnamon and nutmeg pervaded this room. The second small room, Uncle Art's, held a single bed and dresser. Uncle Art was Grandpa's brother, the unmarried uncle who had run the sheep operation on the ranch. He died on April 16, 1951, four years before Grandpa died. I remember his room best for the tobacco cans that he used as spittoons and for the stack of pulp romances stored in one corner.

I Remember

I remember
hopscotch on the sidewalk
sunshine
tall, shady oaks and maples, and
ivy twining along the ground

I remember
satiny rose petals
fragrant and free to hold
their stalks taller than my head
in beds deep with bark mulch

I remember
a tall white house
a large mahogany desk
a wastebasket of thrown away treasures
at Uncle Arthur's in McMinnville

I remember
Aunt Ruby with her crown of braided hair
an apron always covering the dress she wore
her feet shod in neat dark-colored pumps
and when she went out, a hat upon her head

I remember
Dora, who never married
nor had a home of her own,
yet had time for little girls and their dreams
I remember
her box of satin scraps—
jewels of crimson and white
elegant gowns for a doll

I remember
a family not connected
yet always there
a distance of miles hard to bridge in those days

Daddy's Family

Daddy never said much about his childhood in Wisconsin, but I grew up knowing that he was German. I remember him telling us about one winter when snow piled up deep enough to cover the fence posts, with a crust strong enough to hold a team and sleigh. He mentioned ice-skating on a pond and feeding cows. He was born in Beaver Dam, Wisconsin, but spent time near Lowell, on his grandfather Bramer's farm.

During the corn harvest of 1922, when he was eighteen, he left Wisconsin to join his older brothers Arthur and Raymond in Oregon. His father, George Nicholas Schoenberger, died of a heart attack in 1923, leaving Dad's mother Minnie and a sister Dora, who soon followed the boys to Oregon. Arthur, the oldest, settled in McMinnville where he raised two daughters. He and Ruby lived in a two-story white house shaded by tall oaks and maples. On summer visits, I played hopscotch on the front sidewalk in the sunshine with Sheila and Karen, Arthur's granddaughters. Because Arthur was born in 1887 and Dad in 1904, we children were close in age.

Ivy twined along the ground in the shade, but behind the house, I discovered a new playground in Arthur's rose garden. The deep bark mulch lay moist and fragrant under my feet as I lost myself amid roses that were taller than my head. I collected satiny petals, fragrant and fallen—free beauty that I held and savored.

Inside, the house was cool and airy. It had a separate dining room where Aunt Ruby served the meals, a room with Uncle Arthur's large mahogany desk, and a wastebasket of thrown away treasures. There was a real bathroom tucked under the stairway. It held a flush toilet and a claw-footed tub where I could get wet all over.

Aunt Ruby, with her hair braided and wound in a corona around her head, reigned in this house. Instead of a costly robe, she wore a bibbed apron covering her dress, stockings on her legs, and neat, dark pumps on her feet. When she left the house for church or visits, she always wore a hat. As a child, I walked in awe of her—she seemed so much a lady, different from anyone I knew.

Dad's sister Dora spent her life working as a practical nurse at the hospital in McMinnville. She never married, and when I was small, she occupied an upstairs room in Arthur's home. She contained her thin, white hair in a hairnet, and like Ruby, she wore a bibbed apron over her dress.

She had time for little girls and their dreams. In her upstairs room, with sunshine creating patterns through the lace curtains, I would sit on the floor exploring her scrap box. Here I found bits of satin or lace to create gowns for my doll. Aunt Dora would send us Christmas boxes containing crocheted doll outfits or doll blankets made of woven squares, backed and edged with satin and finished with featherstitching.

Uncle Ray, a tall, thin man with sandy hair, wore white short-sleeved shirts and white pants held up by suspenders. He, like Dora, looked like a Bramer while Dad, Arthur, and Ernest resembled the Schoenbergers. Ray, who never married, lived in a small trailer near the McMinnville Hospital where he worked as a janitor.

Grandma Minnie played no part in my life; she died in 1937, before Dad and Mother were married. At that time, she was keeping house for Dad in Mitchell, Oregon, where he was teaching school. My only connection to her is through family photos and a delicate porcelain creamer—quite possibly her mother's—that came from Germany.

Uncle Ernie and his family lived in Wisconsin and were unknown to me except as names on Christmas cards. When Ernie died in March of 1963, Dad felt a need to go back. He had not returned since his arrival in Oregon, but then he felt he had to go. He asked Bud and me to go with him and Mother to help with the straight-through driving that would be required to reach Wisconsin in time for the funeral. The weather made this a harrowing trip. A freezing rain and silver thaw had wrapped the area in layers of ice and snow. Everything, each little blade of grass or stark black twig, glistened beneath a wrapping of crystal. There were no interstate highways yet, so we traveled on snow-packed, two-lane roads.

North of Idaho Falls, Idaho, Dad chose to cross Rabbit Ear Pass, as it was a shorter route. I awoke in the back seat of the Volkswagen with a full moon shining through the window. Tall trees silhouetted against the moonlight cast shadows across the deep snow that covered the road. No snowplow had been here. Bud and Dad put chains on the tires and tried to plow ahead, to no avail. Retreating, we learned that no one kept this highway open in heavy snow. We had to continue, following a longer route.

It was a hard three days of continuous driving as we took turns sleeping in the car, stopping only for gasoline and food. Snippets of mental pictures remain. There were bologna sandwiches fixed in the car and an occasional hamburger grabbed at a fast-food spot. I remember a road in Iowa that twisted from a high bluff down into a valley, where a small white church stood amid a grove of trees whose leafless branches reached up to a wintry sky. We reached Neenah, Wisconsin, in the afternoon of the third day, and I remember having just enough time to freshen up before going to the wake.

Aunt Lulu had a small, two-story home furnished with plain, almost Shaker simplicity. There were oak furnishings, shiny wood floors, and a deep bathtub in an upstairs bath. There was also a boardwalk from the front gate to the porch, and a squirrel feeder off to one side, which Aunt Lulu filled with corn for the local squirrel.

The wake for Uncle Ernie was definitely a new experience. I had been to funerals, always a sorrowful sharing, but this added an entirely different facet to my concept of mourning and paying respect. The immediate family members gathered at the funeral home and were all seated in chairs placed along the sides of the room where the casket was. Friends and acquaintances came and went, viewing the deceased, shaking hands, hugging, and most of all, visiting—sharing anecdotes and memories. Although sorrow was present, the normalcy, the sense of moving ahead that was conveyed in this fashion amazed me. Ernie was gone, but others remained. The caring was for them, to ease their burden and assist them in continuing without him. I went away from the wake with a lighter heart, and the graveside service that took place the following day seemed unnecessary.

For most of the time, there was little contact between that family and mine. We exchanged letters, but money was scarce and the distance between eastern Oregon, McMinnville, and Wisconsin was always an impediment. I knew there was family, but we were not a close-knit tribe that supported each other. Each family unit seemed insular and apart. As each generation grew, I think the trait was reinforced. We are now scattered from the Atlantic to the Pacific—and I have traveled a great portion of the geography yet made contact with few.

Chapter 4: School Days

Memories of my school years are motley with no sense of time or date, but they do retain the flavor of growing up. I attended my first year of school in Spray, Oregon. My teacher gave me *Kerry, The Fire Engine Dog*, a thin book with a bright red cover. She also gave me my first taste of avocado on a saltine cracker. I was not impressed. That year we lived across the main highway from school, next to Cora Argylebright's house. Dad erected a canvas tent-house, as other housing was unavailable. He used that same tent again two years later but in another location. Corie, as everyone called her, had a grey cat, more blue than grey really, that didn't like children. Her daughter teased it by digging at its ribs with a pencil. How cruel that seemed to me.

That same year I had trouble hearing and had terrible earaches throughout the winter. Mother dropped warmed mineral oil into my ear and kept me in bed with my ear on a hot water bottle to ease the pain. Eventually, she and Dad took me to a doctor in McMinnville who blew air into my ears. It hurt fiercely, but then I could hear. Our footsteps on the stairs when we left resounded like thunder in my head. The doctor said I would have to have my tonsils out or I would be deaf within six months.

In the spring, Dad took me to the clinic in John Day for the surgery. I lay on a table while sunshine poured through a window behind my head. The doctor said, "Breathe deeply." Then I couldn't breathe—a mesh cone covered my nose. I was choking and tried to struggle…then I woke up with a sore throat. I was fighting. The sheet trapped my feet, and because I could not free them, I kicked wildly. Finally, I was able to tell someone to unwrap my feet. I was back. I remember thinking that the worst part of the experience was being promised all the ice cream and Coke that I wanted and then not being able to swallow it. The cold of one tiny spoonful of ice cream hurt my throat so much that I did not eat more, and the Coke fizzled and burned as I swallowed.

When I entered the second grade, we lived back at Top, and I attended school in Monument. My teacher, Mrs. Hinton, had a large classroom with lots of windows. I enjoyed the year and helped her drill slower readers in phonics. I was a real dictator. The kids probably hated me. At least I thought they did. I never felt a part of any group—I got along with the other kids, but I was a teacher's daughter, and I was not with the same class every year because Dad did not always stay at the same school.

Back in Spray the following year, we lived in the southeast part of town, but again in the tent-house. The walk to school seemed very long as the road curved through town. We lived on one end of town, and the school was at the other end. The scariest time was

Halloween night when some high school boys followed us in a car. Ruth and I pretended to ignore them, but our feet certainly moved faster.

One day after school, I invited two friends to come home with me. Mother served us tomato juice and crackers for a snack but later said, "Never bring your friends home without asking me first." I never did again.

I also learned a lesson about charge accounts there. Mr. Hopper had a small store where kids liked to go after school. Instead of going straight home one afternoon, as Mother expected me to do, I accompanied the Wight girls to Hopper's. They bought ice cream slices and told Mr. Hopper, "Put them on the account."

"What will you have?" he asked, turning to me.

I had found a bracelet with small charms attached. "This," I told him. "Put it on our account."

Later, Dad asked me, "Carol, do you know what a charge account is?"

"No."

"It's when a store agrees to let you take things on credit without paying because you will pay the bill when you get paid. Do you understand?"

"Uh huh."

Then he asked, "Can you pay for the bracelet?"

"No."

"Well, I don't have an account at Hopper's because I can't afford one. We will have to take the bracelet back."

That was my first lesson in money management.

During the winter, the oil stove was the heart of our home. Mother set her yeast dough in bread pans next to it to rise. Sometimes my cat White Paw would walk across the cloth-covered loaves, leaving his footprints indented into the fresh dough. I cuddled next to the stove to keep warm while reading an endless procession of books, including *Crimson Roses* by Grace Livingston Hill, my favorite of her books; every Zane Grey I could get my hands on, and of course Nancy Drew. Most evenings, Dad would sit on one side of the stove reading aloud to us before we went to bed.

In late May, we moved back to Top without White Paw—a clown at the rodeo grounds had stolen him to use in his act. He needed a cat to put in a suitcase that was then dropped from a bucking horse. Naturally, a tame housecat was ideal, but White Paw was scared and disappeared. I had had him since he was a kitten, and his absence made me sad. Each Sunday after church through that summer, Dad would drive by the rodeo grounds so that I could call for him. About a month later, he came when I called, and I was able to take him home.

That was not the last time White Paw went traveling. He also disappeared from the ranch and wandered halfway to Monument once. I think he was gone a month that time too. Again, Dad found him while driving home in the Jeep. I suppose he was just tomcatting, as I have found out since that most toms do. However, at that time, he just about broke my heart each time he left.

Why? He was my confidant, a shoulder to weep on, a warm purr to lull me to sleep, and a playmate as well. Blackie, his mother, gave birth to her kittens on the foot of my bed, and White Paw was special from the start. We did many things together. I even dressed him (under protest) in doll clothes and tried, unsuccessfully, to keep him in a doll buggy. He was still with us in 1955 when we moved to Kimberly, but then he just disappeared one time too many, not to return.

I recall very little about my fourth and fifth grades, but both were unpleasant. I was at Monument both years. During that time, we had to relearn the Pledge of Allegiance, adding the words "under God." I was never fast at arithmetic, especially flash cards. When the fourth-grade teacher would call my name, my mind would go blank as I tried to figure out the answer. Then, in fifth grade with Mrs. Farrell, I had trouble with fractions. While the other kids in my class clowned around, even climbing onto the window ledge, I tried to make the numbers work. Dad even helped me at home, but I was still frustrated. To this day, I am not fast with figures.

Mirinda Musgrave, my cousin, and Laura Lee Bleakman, her cousin, were in my class. We all rode the bus together. I was jealous because they always wore newer, store-bought clothes. I resented the girls for having things Dad could not afford for me. My dresses were what Mother made, often from printed flour sacks. Some were hand-me-downs too. And how I hated long, brown, cotton stockings and black galoshes with buckles, instead of knee-highs and rain boots for bad weather.

Although I did not realize it at the time, Daddy was a respected teacher in the local area. He was also in demand, although he preferred to farm. It was at this time that Grant County convinced him to accept the grades five through eight position at Izee, a small cattle-ranching and mill-town community in the back of beyond, west of John Day. Like many small communities, it was cattle versus sawmill, and the school kids rarely saw eye-to-eye on anything.

The small white school was located central to the ranches not the mill town, and the school board was dominated by ranchers whose children attended the school. Some of these were second- or third-generation ranchers who had attended the school themselves as children. On the other hand, the people in town were mill employees and their families. They lived in company houses and bought goods from the company store. They were not permanent residents—most only stayed a year or two before moving to another mill. They had short-term interest compared to the long-term ideas of the ranch residents.

There was no housing near the rural school except for one small teacherage, grey and unpainted. Mother and Dad purchased an old eight-by-twenty-six-foot trailer house from Lyle Van Dusen. I look back and wonder how Mom coped. There were five us, plus Shep and two or three cats, only one double bed and a sofa that made down at night. I guess Georgia slept on a cot, but I don't remember. There was no bathroom, only a chamber pot; but then I had never lived in a house with a flushing toilet. The Musgraves had one, and so did Ida Hopper at Spray, so I was familiar with the convenience. Most places, even Grandpa's, still used an outhouse complete with newspaper and catalogs. Anyway, the first year there, Dad hired Miss Hopper to teach grades one through four, and she lived in the teacherage. She had Ruth and Georgia in her classroom that was part of the local grange hall. I went to grade six in Daddy's room in the schoolhouse.

Dad situated our trailer between the grange hall and the school. The teacherage was on the other side of the school building. Sometimes on a clear night, Ruth and I would get in the gully behind Miss Hopper's and yip like coyotes. She hated that! She would yell and scold. I wonder if she realized it was only us girls. We were so convincing one night, that we actually called coyotes in and scared ourselves almost witless. It was on nights like that with a full moon that we could see deer grazing no more than fifty yards from the trailer. They would come out of the sage and juniper hills to eat what little grass grew in the small valley where the school was located.

I physically became a woman that year and started noticing the boys. At that age, the boys were embarrassed, and so was I. We girls would secrete our personal notes and cast sidelong looks at the boys, but rarely did the two sexes meet—except at sporting events or, for a rare few of the girls, on dates.

Mostly, I remember how Dad would read aloud to us each day after lunch. Zane Grey came alive with *Wildfire*. He also read other books that I have forgotten until I run across one and again hear his voice echo across the years. I was always a reader, but his reading aloud at home and at school deepened my love for books. As a teacher, he was always patient and gentle. (I wish I could say the same about me!) While reading, he would sit on one corner of his desk with the sun glancing off his hair, by then touched with grey. His low voice held us spellbound for at least thirty minutes.

I always entered the school through the back door, leaving my coat on a hook in the cloakroom. A bookcase stood to the right just inside the classroom. I read most of the books including *Brighty of Grand Canyon, Big Red*, and all of the Nancy Drew books. Windows in the left wall opened up the room, flooding it with light. The oil stove stood centered against the right wall. Between the stove and the windows, four rows of desks—one for each grade—lined up like soldiers at attention. Each desk had a lift-up top and storage space for books and supplies. Dad's desk stood in the right front corner, with one window beside and one behind it in the front wall. A second window on the left balanced the wall. A door centered between them opened onto a porch and a playground with two teeter-totters.

Each class, beginning with grade five on the left, had its own row. Dad would go over the lesson for one grade, and while those students worked, he would move on to another grade. He always helped us when we had problems, but he answered our questions with other questions until we finally answered our own question. I later learned that this was the Socratic Method, and I used it with my students who always hated it, but it helped them learn to think. When we finished our work, we could read or work on something else. I spent lots of time on a geography project and drawing.

Even then, I was competitive. One of the boys could draw horses that galloped off his paper. I began by tracing their outlines from horse magazines. My horses did not run, let alone gallop. They were stiff, without life. But I persisted. When the school received new cedar siding, I picked up the scraps and painted pictures on them using tempera colors. Because I kept drawing and painting, Mother and Dad bought me a set of oil paints for Christmas. My first oil painting was of a grey burro against a green background, painted on a scrap of cedar siding.

In the spring of my sixth-grade year, the Game Commission sponsored a writing contest with a topic on wildlife conservation. I wrote an essay about beavers and their contribution to the land. I won first prize for my grade level in Grant County and received a check for $5.00. This was my first attempt as a writer.

I had two good friends at Izee, Kay Shuckle and Peggy Ellis, both from the mill town. We shared much. Kay was from a large Catholic family, and although Mother was friendly with Kay's mother, she thought that as Catholics, they were damned. The pope ruled them; they confessed to priests for forgiveness—how could any man remove sin from another—and they did not pray to God. Peggy, on the other hand, was the only child in her home. She was a large girl but pretty with short, curly blond hair, and I envied her for her privileges. She had her own room, wore makeup, cut her hair, went to movies, and stayed up as late as she wanted. She was a year older than I was, and all grown up.

The second year we were there, we had to move the trailer down behind the teacherage. I do not remember why. Miss Hopper said, "I can't stand another year of kids." Dad had to find someone else to take her place with grades one through four. The replacement was a real Tartar. I never saw her laugh or say a kind word to any of the children. She would chase us away from her house for being too noisy, and she even browbeat her poor husband. I do not believe anyone liked her.

Looking back, I see two women, both retired, coaxed back into the classroom because of need. It was difficult for out-of-the-way rural schools to find teachers willing to spend nine months away from homes and town conveniences. Knowing how I responded to students as I entered my fifties, I am sure that Miss Hopper left Izee emotionally drained and physically exhausted after her time spent with the six- to ten-year-olds. The second teacher went through the motions, but I am sure that she resented being there. We children felt all of that.

That winter, we belly-flopped on our sleds and sped down the hill toward the road—not the greatest idea, but we survived. I even tried standing up. That was centuries ago! I cannot even imagine doing that now. In addition, Mother taught me to crochet and to embroider. I began a large pink-and-purple pineapple doily that became my *bête noire*. How many times it was ripped out and redone, I do not recall, but it never did lie flat. Now I know why. The pattern omitted one entire pineapple and joining. This made the center into a dish instead of a flat piece. Oh well, I did learn to make the stitches.

I also fell in love with mushroom soup and rice that year. It is still a favorite—a comfort food that is good when nothing else appeals. Peggy would bring a can of soup, and Mom would add the rice, making hot soup for lunch. Dad shot his first and only deer that fall because we needed meat. Winter was so cold that he hung the carcass and let it freeze. I do not remember Mom packaging any of it. With no freezer, they just let it hang and used off it when needed.

I saw the planet Jupiter in the night sky that winter when the nights were so clear and cold that the sky was blue. When I would go outside to the outhouse, I could see Jupiter overhead, as large as a softball but bright like a star. I saw it again that clear and bright the winter of 1997. I really think that living in eastern Oregon has something to do with what I see. Here, there is space. Here is the desert without city lights. The heavens seem to lie much closer, and the stars loom much brighter than anywhere else that I have lived.

Dad decided to quit teaching that year, and he and Mother decided to sell the ranch at Top. Dad said it was getting harder each year to cope with the schoolchildren, and for retirement he wanted something else. Jack Forrest, who lived on the North Fork of the John Day River below our place, bought the ranch to enlarge his holdings, and we girls were delighted when Dad decided to buy the Texaco Station at Kimberly.

As Dad had always liked to work with cars or in his shop, he looked forward to the mechanical aspect of the business.

This was the spring of 1955. Dad had turned fifty-one. We were leaving the sticks and moving to town, even if it was only a highway junction. I was young and ready to fly, and I had met Bud Crandell. At that time, Frank and Wilma Crandell, his parents, lived in Spray. Frank pastored the Missionary Baptist Church, where our family attended. Bud helped Dad move the livestock that had to be loaded and trucked to Kimberly. Bud, Ruth, and I drove them on foot up to the road where they were loaded. Then we all rode the truck to Kimberly. I thought Bud was nice. He was tall, had dark brown hair that he wore brushed into a flip like the one Elvis had, and was an "older man" attending Oregon Technical Institute in Klamath Falls.

This was a time to change. I was growing up in a new environment, meeting all sorts of people. Two women vacationing from Texas stopped for gas and a rest break under the shade of the Chinese elms. There were young men with the state highway department, older men who came for the fishing, not-so-old men from the ranches who saw a pretty face. There were those who paid their bills, and those who did not. As schoolchildren, we now rode the big yellow school bus for nineteen miles to Monument. This was the river run that Ernie Johnson drove. In the winter, my feet did get cold! To top it off, girls dressed like girls then. We wore skirts and sweaters with saddle oxfords or penny loafers. There were no jeans, slacks, or nylons—only bobby sox. There were a few days of biting cold when rules were bent enough to allow the extra layer of nylons, but not very often. At that, it was nice to have a bus stop right outside the door instead of a mile away, and I did not miss the walk through mud or snow from the ranch house to the road.

My eighth-grade year at Monument presented a few surprises. The kids that I had been with off and on through grade school only wanted to play. I tried to study. They were interested in dating and all the extracurricular events. I was interested but not much of a participant. When you live nineteen miles from school and do not dance or go to movies, a boy asks you out only once because, even though he likes you, he wants a companion, and those are the only activities available. It was the same way later in high school.

Mr. Gertsen taught grades seven and eight. In a way, I think most of us were a bit afraid of him. He was nice, but he would tolerate little nonsense. His standard threat was: "I'll fall on you." This would have been disastrous as he was over six feet tall and seemed just as immense in girth.

Several things stand out about that school year. I broke my habit of chewing my nails—I had promised myself a new purse if I could do it, and I did. This was the year that Lydia Capon, the high school home economics teacher, suggested that I needed a deodorant. I was mortified. Mother had never said a word! This was the year my subjects came easily for me. I was academically ahead of others in my class, so Dad let me spend time with the Van Dusens when their new baby arrived. I was valedictorian of my class at graduation, even though there was some strong argument from those who thought I should not be, as I had not attended Monument every year. Mr. Gertsen did not waver, however, and I wrote my speech, with its closure: "If God be for us, who can be against us?" and delivered it for the class. This was the second piece that I remember writing.

The next step, into ninth grade in high school, was a big one. Like the other kids, I questioned my ability to succeed "upstairs." Yet the time came, and I coped. Freshman initiation could have been worse. We had to dress in wrong-side-out clothes, backward dresses, or a diaper with baby bottle, among other things, and upperclassmen painted our faces with red lipstick. Then they blindfolded us and lined us up in the cafeteria where they fed us such things as peeled grapes or slimy spaghetti, but the worst was the chunk of raw onion placed on my tongue. Because I cannot tolerate the taste, it almost made me sick, and I could not swallow it.

Somehow I survived. I was a flop in sports: my

volleyball serve was weak with erratic placement; my swing in baseball was hesitant; and even though I could run, I could not catch the ball—I broke a finger instead. On the other hand, I was a good team manager for girls' volleyball, earned my school letter, and kept a mean set of stats for basketball.

I excelled in academics even though Junie, our cow, ate the biology notes that I needed to study for an important test. Because our front yard was Highway 19, and the backyard under the elms was bare dirt, I had taken my sheaf of notes to the pasture where I could lie on the grass in the sunshine while I tried to memorize biology terms and facts. I knew Junie was grazing nearby, but she caught me by surprise anyway—her long tongue flicked out and snatched loose pages. When I grabbed for them, she tossed her pointy horns and turned her head away as she continued to chew my papers into mushy pulp.

I had moved upstairs to the high school, but Ruth remained behind in the elementary. As I became involved in separate activities, we began to grow apart. At home, I needed quiet time alone to sort through my feelings. She resented this deeply and showed it by teasing me. One day, she baited me to the point that I picked up a knife. (At least, that is what she told me years later.) I do not remember that, but I do recall taking after her with a stick of stove wood when she kept grabbing and picking at my embroidery stitching.

"I was mean and rotten to get you to stop being quiet and spend time with me," she told me years later. I always thought that she had gotten into my trunk and lost the ruby ring given to me by Uncle Larry. Instead, my younger sister Georgia lost it. Ruth found it caught in the cobwebs between the wall studs where Dad had not yet hung plywood.

I worked very hard to complete high school in three years instead of four. It is difficult to separate my memories of those high school years into distinct periods, however. There certainly were highlights, but much of the time was a routine of classes and study. In the fall, one of the teachers always had a radio playing so no one would miss the World Series games. This same radio announced the moment when the first Russian Sputnik shot off into space. Most classes were rather relaxed. Mr. Crombie, however, liked to crack the whip, especially in Western Civilization class. He would stride into the room, ordering us to, "Take out a sheet of paper. Put your name, period, and date on it." Then came four essay questions, each worth twenty-five points. In this way, he made sure that we had read our material. He was small in stature, not over five-foot-four. He wore his blond hair brushed sideways to cover a balding head, and his eyes snapped behind heavy-framed glasses. He reminded me of a cocky bantam rooster, but he wore tan tweed suits with pinstripe shirts and ties instead of bright shiny feathers. We were uncomfortable around him.

There were others. Mr. Drees was a tall man with black hair beginning to grey at the temples; he dressed in dark pants with a sports jacket and was casual about his appearance. He was also forgetful and quite disorganized. As his secretary, I learned to decipher his scrawl—more or less. His signature was a D followed by a line. Besides that, I recorded the daily student attendance, took lunch money, and punched lunch tickets.

All of us loved Coach McVey. He cared about us whether we were in his science class or on the gym floor. I even babysat for him a couple of times.

Days at Monument High varied little. The school was small—at that time, all twelve grades were in one rectangular, two-storied building. The high school had three rooms on the second floor. There was a large homeroom where everyone had a desk—the antique type with wrought iron legs bolted to the floor, fold-up seats, and generations of initials and names carved into the dark wooden tops. Everyone shared a cloakroom that provided hooks on the walls for hanging up coats. Typing class was in a tiny narrow room that had barely enough space to work. Then there was the science room with one sink and a Bunsen burner set-up. Home economics took place in the cafeteria, and physical education was outside or in the gym. One winter the gym burned, and we finished the basketball season playing on borrowed floors.

My last year of school was the fullest year and, perhaps, the best remembered. The preceding summer, three boys from Portland had attempted to run the John Day River in a canoe. Harold Hinds, Lee Bouchard, and Larry Sall capsized and demolished their canoe on the rapids below our place at Kimberly. As a result, they spent several weeks with us before their parents could bring a rubber raft to them from Portland so that they could continue their run downriver to the Columbia. All three boys attended high schools in the Portland area and were basically city fellers. Thus, even though they enjoyed the country, they became quite bored when stuck in the middle of nowhere, sixty miles from a major town and a movie.

To help pass the time, they went rattlesnake hunting. They wanted to take live rattlers back to the zoo in Portland. This was quite an experience for me. I had grown up knowing that rattlesnakes were dangerous, and my sole concern was to avoid them. Now, I was included in a search to capture them. The boys always proceeded with caution. They used a pole approximately six feet long with a thong or heavy string affixed to one end. The string was secured along one side so that it formed a loop that they slipped over the snake's head and drew tight without the handler having to be within striking distance. Once the snakes were caught, the boys stuffed them into a burlap bag and later housed them in wood and wire cages. The boys sometimes loosed the snakes and displayed them for travelers who stopped by. This brought them a little extra money.

In addition to snake catching, all three boys enjoyed swimming. The river behind our place had an excellent spot, dredged deep by the highway commission when they needed gravel. The boys spent hours there on hot summer afternoons. Even though they tried to teach me, I never successfully learned how to swim.

I became friends with Harold and Lee, but for some reason I was never comfortable with Larry. Before school started in the fall, I was able to spend a week with both Harold's and Lee's families in Portland. This was my first real experience with a big city. The traffic and size of the place amazed me. I stayed up until two in the morning, watching television—something I had never experienced before. Because I liked to sew, Lee's mother took me to Sears in the Lloyd Center where she worked and allowed me to select dress fabric. I saw fabrics in so many varied colors and textures that I had a difficult time selecting only one. Finally, I chose a blue-green knit that I later made into a sack dress with three-quarter sleeves and a cowl collar.

My friendships with Harold and Lee were long-lasting. Lee returned to Kimberly for deer season for several years and by the early nineties, had settled into a home in Fossil, Oregon. Harold went off to college and eventually to the University of Chicago. We kept in touch with letters, Christmas cards, and rare visits if we happened to be in the same place at the same time. I saw Harold briefly when he was at home in Portland. Then he stopped in Spokane when he was returning to the University of Chicago. He married Liz, attended graduate school at Vanderbilt University, and later spent time in Latin America researching for his doctoral work. Eventually, they settled in Morris, Minnesota, where he held a teaching position at the university there. Liz obtained her law degree and practiced in St. Paul.

In addition to making new friends my senior year, I took a correspondence course in photo tinting and was involved in more activities at school. This was the year that I helped in the office, worked as a library aide, and was chosen as art editor for the yearbook and the newspaper. I enjoyed all of these activities and stayed busy with them and my schoolwork. I was also doubling on English and taking American History by correspondence so that I could finish in three years instead of the traditional four. I did well in both subjects, in addition to keeping up my regular classes. When graduation came, however, I was unable to be a speaker because I was a three-year graduate. Instead, the school board honored me with an award for achievement to acknowledge that I had earned the highest grade point average of all who were graduating in 1959.

I thought other students liked me, yet I was never close to anyone. The small groups of girls would quit talking if I came near, and the boys clammed up with their jokes. I had the impression that they talked about things I was not supposed to know about. Besides, I did not date and I did not swear. I was too different.

During basketball season, students provided sandwiches and cocoa for players after the game. It was my turn to serve at one of the home games, and I was setting up in the cafeteria when Daddy came to tell me he needed to leave early. Could I find a ride home? Naturally, I was concerned that something was wrong at home. He kept saying that nothing was wrong, but he had to leave. Eventually, I noticed the twinkle in his eyes and knew he was trying to keep something from me. He finally admitted that Mother had phoned the school to say Bud was coming by bus to Prineville, where Dad was to meet him at ten o'clock. I talked Dad into letting me go with him and found one of the girls to swap kitchen duty with me.

Because it was December, the temperature was cold. I do not remember snow on the ground unless there was some in the Ochoco Mountains. Along the John Day River, the weather was usually mild, although there were times when a twelve-inch snowfall would surprise us. This particular night the temperature was low enough that I wore a heavy coat and the heater in the Jeep station wagon kept my feet toasty warm.

Bud had been in Guam for sixteen months, and no one was expecting him home for Christmas 1958. He had been told that there was absolutely no chance at all for him to be stateside early, so he took leave for Japan. Somehow, though, there was an Operation Santa Claus that would have brought him home if proper papers had been processed. When he returned from Japan, he learned of this and was able to pull strings and get his papers cleared. This brought him home before reassignment at Fairchild AFB in Spokane, Washington, where he would finish his four-year tour of duty.

At this time, Bud was a friend on paper as I had been writing to him for two years. Bud had stayed with us that summer of 1955 while he worked in the apple orchard earning money to return to college. He then returned to OTI and graduated in May 1956—the same time I graduated from the eighth grade. By this time, his parents had moved to Dayton, Washington, to run a Richfield service station. Bud opened the station and spent a month there before his dad could take over. Then, he and a friend drove to Spokane and enlisted in the air force. He left his car with Dad to sell, I think. Before she moved, his mother asked me to write to Bud because her glasses were bad and she needed new ones; therefore, she said, she could not see to write well. I did not mind writing to him for her, as I rather liked him by that time. I wrote long letters each week to update him on everything going on. He wrote me a short letter every six or seven weeks.

Now it was December 18, 1958, and he was on his way home. Romantic notions and many questions filled my thoughts. How would he feel about me? He was coming to my home first—what did that mean? Come to find out, the Greyhound bus drivers were going out on strike. From California, he had taken the train to Klamath Falls where he stopped to see if his sister Carol and her husband were home; they had already left to drive north to Dayton, Washington, for the holiday. Rather than take a bus, he hitchhiked, catching a truck headed straight through to Portland. Unfortunately, the weather was bad, and by the time they reached the Highway 58 junction to Eugene, the trucker decided to go that way and over the Willamette Pass. This left Bud and a swabbie stranded out in a blizzard, wearing dress uniforms without topcoats. They waited two hours before another truck stopped. This got Bud to Redmond, where the last bus was just leaving. He caught it and met us at the Ochoco Inn in Prineville at midnight, two hours later than expected. As he came up the steps and across the room to catch me close in his arms, I knew I loved him.

Bud was so chilled that Dad turned the heater to high, I put my heavy coat around him, and he slept all the way to Kimberly. Worst of all, he developed tonsillitis and was flat in bed for three days. Luckily, our neighbor, Effie Stirewalt, had an antibiotic on hand and gave Mother some of the capsules. They helped, and he improved. We were going to drive him to Dayton, but the station wagon developed problems. Finally, Bud phoned his sister Carol and her husband Bill to come after him. Carol later told me that she had wondered why he was at Kimberly instead of some place closer to Dayton, but when she saw the two of us together, she knew.

Bud had a thirty-day leave before he had to report for duty in Spokane, so I saw him several times during January. He drove his dad's old truck down, even though it was so riddled with problems that it was a miracle it held together. We would take that old truck for a drive and then find a place to park. There were several convenient places, including nearby gravel pits. We used them all. I was surprised that when we would come home at two or four in the morning, my parents said nothing. Like most young couples, we spent our time talking and petting. It was one such night that Bud gave me a silver heart with a Bali dancer etched onto the smoked background. I wore it constantly.

In February, he called and asked me to marry him at Easter. I agreed. When I told his mother, she said, "You're jumping from the frying pan into the fire." As she said nothing more, I did not understand. In March when the seniors went to Pendleton for senior pictures, I met him at the Temple Hotel for a milkshake and came away with his Mitchell High School class ring. It was several sizes too large, but with adhesive tape, glitter, and nail polish, I made it fit. I wore it to school and created quite a stir. The quiet little mouse was the first to plan a wedding. When word got around that we had set an Easter date, the talk began. I did not realize until later what students were saying, but Ruth told me one night at home.

One particular day, I wore a pale lavender, cotton skirt to school, and my period started. Before I realized it, a bright red stain decorated the back of my skirt. Not knowing, I went to get keys from Mr. Drees in the science room so that I could get lunch money and be on duty in the cafeteria. As I left his classroom and closed the door, I saw the red stain on my skirt reflected in the glass door panes. Mirinda loaned me her long coat and had her mother bring a pair of bright orange pedal pushers for me to wear for the rest of the day. Did Mother ever have a fit when I arrived home wearing those. The pants disgraced her. She was not concerned about why I had worn them, only that I had. Ruth said that some of the girls had been saying that I had to get married, and when I left the classroom, their faces were beet red. That was one sure way to squelch a rumor, even though my face was red with embarrassment too.

Shortly after that, I found out just how many friends I really had. The girls at school and Mrs. Gertsen (the former Lydia Capon, English and home economics teacher) planned a surprise shower for me; Bess Foree, friend and neighbor, hosted another shower; and best wishes came from all sides. I was not the only one disappointed when we had to postpone the wedding because complications arose about Bud's getting leave at Easter time.

I finished high school on May 20, and my family and I left for Dayton on the twenty-third. When we arrived is immaterial, but the afternoon hours spent with Bud after he talked to Daddy were special to me. When he finally asked Daddy if he could marry me, Dad chuckled softly and said, "I wondered if you two weren't getting the cart before the horse." After that, we drove into the hills outside of town. To this day, I do not know where we went, but the day was sunny and we ended up down along a creek bordered by overhanging trees and green grass. Sometime that afternoon Bud gave me an engagement ring of white gold with a center-mounted diamond flanked by two small diamonds on each side—five diamonds in all.

Part II
Growing Pains

Living is Risking

Permit me to tell you about living.
Each new day brings a new start
As yesterday fades
And tomorrow dawns.

Mistakes are chances to grow,
To change ideas,
To see in new ways.
But one thing I've learned,
Growing is painful:
It demands action.

Actions come from decisions
That create change.
Living is risking.

Chapter 5: Beginnings

On May 26, 1959, Bud and I were married at the Crandell home on Park Street in Dayton, Washington. It was half-way between Bud at Fairchild AFB and Kimberly where I lived. I wore a lace dress that Bud had bought for me in Walla Walla. I had planned to wear the white satin dress that I had made for graduation, but I wore his dress instead as he said he was buying it whether I wore it or not. Instead of a bouquet, I wore a corsage of pink baby roses. Ruth stood beside me in a pale yellow dress. Bud wore his dress blues, and Bill Hood, his brother-in-law, was his best man. Bud's father, who had performed the ceremony for both of his daughters' church weddings, married us in a very brief ceremony.

I had been awake since six that morning, but had not been allowed out of the bedroom for fear someone would see me. Thus, I had eaten nothing. The ceremony was at nine, and we left shortly after cutting the cake. Bud had purchased a car, a light blue Plymouth, and someone had carefully decorated it so that we could clean it quickly—however, we never did get all the rice out of the interior. In the backseat, I discovered a box of essential groceries that Carol Lee, Bud's sister, had prepared. We stopped for dinner, but by then I was too hungry to eat and felt sick enough that I only picked at my food. Besides, I was extremely nervous.

We began married life in a small apartment with three rooms and a bath. Bud was doing janitorial work there in exchange for the apartment. The private bath cost him $7.50 each month, but it was better than sharing the communal bath for that hall. The apartment building was of brick construction and not bad for its time. It was clean but always seemed dark, especially as ours was an inside apartment with only one window that opened onto an inner court. The tiny living room had an overstuffed sofa and chair, a small table with four chairs, a desk, an end table, and a radiator. The galley kitchen contained an apartment-sized gas range, a sink, a refrigerator, and a short counter with an overhead cupboard for dishes and supplies. I baked every week but was always afraid to light the oven because it inevitably whooshed at me.

The bathroom with its deep, claw-footed tub, toilet, and washbasin seemed luxurious to me. Dad had never finished the bathroom at home as he'd intended, so I really enjoyed the convenience of a full, working bath just off the bedroom. Our bedroom was larger than the other rooms and could have been rented as a separate unit as it had its own door into the hall. This room held a double bed with a brown metal frame similar to the bed I had slept in at home, a dresser, and two nightstands. A man who sat and rocked all night rented the room directly above our bedroom. I would lie in bed listening to the squeak of his chair rockers on the wooden floor.

Marriage took a great deal of adjustment on my part. To start with, I had to pretend that we were not newlyweds. When Bud applied for the janitorial job at the apartment house, he had told the owner he was married but that his wife was still in school, implying that I was attending college. Besides that, I had long daytime hours to fill, alone, as it took barely an hour to clean the tiny apartment. I discovered the city library within walking distance, and during the summer I read books by the armful. I walked some, exploring the area close to us, but it was not long before boredom set in. Finally, Bud agreed that I could look for a job. Then I learned how little I was prepared for the world in which I lived. I did not have experience enough for any job, but especially the photo studios where I tried to get coloring work. Eventually, I obtained temporary clerical work with an insurance company. My job required lots of filing, some typing, and other very basic clerical tasks. In November, I quit to move to the Earl Apartments, where Bud and I had taken the managerial position.

By now, I had faced up to the reality that Bud smoked occasionally and swore more frequently. This really bothered me, as I had been raised in a nonsmoking, no swearing home. To my dismay, I was learning that he was, after all, a man—a GI in all senses of the term, not just a preacher's son. I guess I had idealized him in a romantic way and had never really known him casually enough to see him as a human being. I had much to learn.

Living at the Earl occupied more of my time, as I was responsible for the mail, answering the phone, renting apartments, and keeping the halls clean. I did the halls daily, the bathrooms weekly, and apartments whenever they became vacant. Some of them were real messes. The kitchens were the worst with dirt, grease, and sometimes food splattered on the walls and cupboards. At that time, I did not have my favorite cleaner named 409, so I spent lots of time scrubbing with hot water and cleanser. There were cobwebs and dust rolls, stained sinks, dirty floors, and dusty carpets. Some rooms would take me an entire day to make presentable. It amazed me how other people, especially the single men, could let their quarters get so dirty.

A girl from Kamiah, Idaho, moved into the room above our bedroom. She was older than I was, and she was different from anyone I had ever known. Her hair was naturally reddish, but she dyed it with henna until it looked like rich, dark mahogany. She was not exactly pretty, but she was put together nicely and had an animal magnetism about her that attracted the guys. She was not really a "bad girl," as they were called in 1959, but she was friendly; she would take in anyone as one would a lost puppy, even if that person ended up in her bed. We became friends, as we both had time to spare. Some afternoons we played rummy; others we just talked. She introduced me to cabbage and tuna as a salad. She also taught me a great deal about life.

I was mature for seventeen, but I was also very naive. By listening to her and to her friends when they dropped in, I discovered that you did not have to be married to want or like sex. They did not even feel guilty about it! She also gave me some inkling of what men really wanted from women. We talked girl talk, and she gave me a sounding board and an ear when I was confused or sometimes did not understand Bud. He and I were still learning about each other, and there were times, I think, when we both wondered why we had ever gotten married. He would come home wanting a bath, dinner, and an evening of television, while I had spent my day in the apartment building and wanted to go out. I read books, painted a landscape at sunset and Cathedral Rock on the John Day River, and began to research my family history by writing to relatives. Lena Wiley, a long-time resident at the Earl Apartments, sparked my interest. She had grown up in New England and still had a history book that mentioned her family and her by name. She encouraged me to record what information I could gather from living relatives. Occasionally, Bud and I would attend a movie at the Fox Theater downtown or the drive-in. We would drive somewhere or go shopping on weekends. We seemed to spend a lot of time looking at cars.

The Plymouth aggravated Bud with a squeak that he could not find. He finally traded it for a forest green Volkswagen. I thought the Bug was ugly, but I liked the Renault Dauphin he was considering even less.

Actually, that Bug was perhaps one of the best buys we ever made from the standpoint of mileage and performance, and it was only the first of a long line of cars that passed through our lives.

Christmas of 1959 was a big event for me. I chose each gift or created one especially for the recipient, wrapped them carefully, and then mailed them off. Afterward I realized that, although it was fun to give lavishly, the chore of paying off the balance on the Sears charge card was no fun at all. I never again put my Christmas expense on a charge account. Lesson three in money management. (The second was learning to manage a checkbook—balanced exactly to the penny.) For Christmas dinner, I selected a twenty-two-pound turkey and all the traditional trimmings. Then I spent a week baking. I was up early Christmas morning to get the turkey in the oven, and by the time I spent the morning preparing dinner, I was almost too tired to enjoy it with Bud and his friend Billy Vowels who had joined us for the day. That turkey fed us for almost a month.

In the spring of 1960, Bud switched from days to nights at work. He was on duty for three or four days around the clock and then off for an equal amount of time. This gave us time to visit Manito Park, the shopping centers, and the Natatorium, an amusement park with a roller coaster. I rode it once, but never again! Sometimes we would drive to Colville where his parents had relocated or back to Kimberly to see mine.

When Bud took his discharge from the air force, we moved back to Kimberly. Dad asked us to run the service station since he had accepted a teaching position at Mitchell for the 1960–61 school year. We did not have many things in our small, furnished apartment, but even without furniture, we had acquired more than the Volkswagen could hold in one trip. Dad returned to Spokane with Bud to get the rest of our things. When they returned, I saw a large collie sitting on Dad's lap. That is how Lady entered our lives.

Both Bud and I had wanted a pet, but we were only able to have parakeets in the apartment. So Dad and Bud visited the animal shelter in Spokane before coming home, and there she sat, a fully grown aristocrat of a collie. Her coat had gone unbrushed for months and was badly matted. Her pants were so woolly and matted that I clipped them. Even so, when I finally got her brushed out, I could not tell where I had clipped and where I had not as she had a long, thick coat. Lady was a gold-and-white collie, but instead of having the white slash on her face that is typical of many collies, she had a perfectly formed black mask above her eyes. Her name, the only one she would respond to, suited her very well. She was dainty in manner and movement. Her four white feet twinkled and danced. I do not believe that she ever plodded. When she ate, she would clean up the edge of her bowl and every scrap that went onto the floor before she would eat from the bowl itself. Her favorite food was spaghetti, and she would come to the kitchen from wherever she was when she caught the first whiff of sauce cooking.

Lady had the natural instincts of a herd dog, but all she had to work with were baby chicks, kittens, the sheep, and a few cows. She accompanied whoever went outside. She chased deer out of the alfalfa field, attended to the milking, or simply supervised whatever activity was underway. When Sandra Jo, Ruth's oldest child, was born, Lady guarded her jealously.

**

At some point during this time, both my father and Bud's father talked about emigrating to Canada. Frank had fished in British Columbia and wanted to live there. Dad liked the idea, but he hesitated. That would be a major upheaval for Mother and him, and Georgia was still in school. They owned property, a business, and animals. It would take time to sell all of that and prepare to move north. Bud was excited about the idea of moving, and we took a trip as far north as Prince George and as far west as Vanderhoof, British Columbia. The southern part of British Columbia was much like Washington. After all, the geography did not change just because humans imposed a border. Near Osoyoos and Penticton, the river valley was green with numerous orchards. Farther north, I thought the scenery comparable to the Columbia River Gorge. The river ran wide and quiet, dark cobalt in color, reflecting the steep rocky sides of the mountains that stood with their feet in the water. At the northern extreme of our trip, we entered a region of lodge-pole pine and lakes. This was moose country. Mosquitoes also inhabited this region. I've never seen such huge ones, either before or since. The road from Prince George to Kamloops was unpaved and very rough. It was a challenge to evade the potholes that seemed to be the road. We drove slowly and with extreme caution, while the native Canadians flew past at seventy miles per hour, throwing dust and gravel in all directions.

For the time we were in Canada, we stayed with a woman named Grace. She was American by birth but had lived in Canada for many years. Her hair was short and silver, her figure quite large but camouflaged by an unending selection of muumuus. She was a widow, but she enjoyed life and people immensely; she had a wide circle of friends. She belonged to a lodge, and while we were there, she took me (I drove) to a dance. No, we didn't dance, but we went to hear the performance of a school fife-and-drum corps dressed in tartan and plaid. They were precision and poetry in motion. The dance began shortly after, and we watched the dancers for a brief time. The ladies in full swirling skirts and spiky high heels floated like thistledown on the arms of their partners as the band played a waltz. One couple in particular was outstanding. The woman wore a pale blue gown with matching heels that hardly seemed to touch the floor as she slid, spun, and pirouetted at the tip of her partner's outstretched arm.

Like Grace, the people of Vanderhoof were open and friendly. They were generous with advice and conversation. They were, however, never in a hurry; there was always tomorrow. They projected a sense of leisure, a timelessness that was in direct contrast to the hurried pace that keeps most Americans from savoring the little joys of life.

Bud and I were seriously considering a move to that region of Canada if we could find property and/or jobs to our liking. We visited an old log cabin near a lake. It certainly had few possibilities for an immediate home: the sod-covered roof had fallen in, there was no floor, and I could not stand erect inside. Even so, I guess it appealed to the pioneer streak deep within me. The only thing I didn't like were the mosquitoes that blanketed the marshy area between the cabin and the lake.

Another place that we explored was thirty miles from Vanderhoof, along the bank of a river that followed lazily along one boundary of the property. Because we were there in the early spring, the ground was still wet and the river high and muddy. To reach the acreage, we left the paved roads of town and followed a narrow muddy track out into the boondocks of lodge pole and scrub. The last mile or two was too deeply rutted in mud for us to attempt with the car; therefore, we walked. We had to go through the neighbor's corral of poles that was erected across the access to the property.

As the day was warm and the trees were just starting to leaf out, the walk was pleasant despite the mud. This parcel of land was nicely situated—partly meadow and partly lodge-pole timber, somewhat higher in elevation above the river at the foot of the property. The house, such as it was, stood on flat ground, not far from the river yet not in the woods. There were no redeeming log walls or rock hearths. Instead, I saw rough lumber and tar paper thrown into a small, single-walled structure that allowed the spring breeze to pass freely between the cracks and through the glassless window. The floor was littered with trash—evidence of a previous occupant— and the acrid droppings of mice and squirrels that now ran at will through the small rooms. There was no water or electricity installed. Instead, a spring and an outhouse were situated close by. In fact, they were located side by side, a few steps from the back door. Worst of all, just outside the rear door, I found a heap of rusty tins, and just beyond that, a moose head, the flesh alive and crawling with maggots. That was the last straw. I could have adjusted to the isolation, the mud, the inconvenience, and even the living quarters, but the filth was too much. I told Bud that I would want an apartment in town. I did not want to live in this place.

Looking back, I wonder what would have happened had I been agreeable to the situation. The land was good, and two thousand dollars was a very reasonable price. If the trash and filth had not been there, the place would have been better. Did I botch up an opportunity, a chance of a lifetime? Certainly, our lives would have followed a different pattern, and neither of us would be the same. I would never have gone to college or become a teacher. Bud, no doubt, would not have become a union carpenter. Would we have had children? Probably. Might we have had a simpler, happier life? Only God knows.

One other time, a year or two later, I returned to Vanderhoof, this time to a job in a dry-goods store, while Bud remained in the states. He still wanted to emigrate and hoped that if I had a job, the way would open. I traveled north on a Greyhound bus and eventually returned the same way. This, in itself, was an adventure. People were pleasant, and most of the time the person in the seat beside me had interesting stories to relate about the places we passed. In Prince George, the boss's son met me and loaded my luggage and me into a tan Volkswagen. Then, like most natives, he barreled his way west, heedless of potholes or the ever-present road construction. Gravel flew and dust boiled into an obscuring cloud behind us. He did deliver me safely to Grace's home, though at times I had my doubts we would make it.

I enjoyed my work and Grace, who fed me well for the price I paid for room and board. Unfortunately, the store's accountant could find no way to get around government and employment red tape. As I was not yet a legal resident of British Columbia, there were problems. In the end, I received a month's wages and bus fare back home. I had been there all of two weeks, part of which was a holiday.

**

Bud and I both enjoyed the time we spent at Kimberly during the winter of 1960, but the service station did not provide the living Bud expected. In the spring of 1961, we moved to Northport, Washington. On one of the several trips that it took us to move, Bud spotted a black Kharman Ghia on a used-car lot in Spokane. The body style was racier than that of the Bug, and we both liked it. Even though the price was $900, an astronomical debt to my way of thinking, we bought it. This car brought with it a sense of adventure. The night that we took possession of the Ghia, we were en route from Kimberly to Northport with a Bug full of belongings. The car salesman simply shook his head in amazement when he saw us. He did not believe that we could get everything we had with us into the Ghia, especially since we had removed the rear seat in the Bug for added space. It was like putting a puzzle together, but we managed to find a place for every item, including the parakeet's cage. It sat on my lap! On a later trip, we brought the rear seat of the Bug to the salesman so that he'd have a complete car to resell.

In Northport, Bud fell timber with a big McCulloch chainsaw, and I helped his mother in the coffee shop. I enjoyed the customers who stopped on their way to or from Canada, but we lived in one upstairs room of his parents' home instead of a place of our own. That lasted for the summer. Then it was back to Kimberly.

In the fall of 1961, Bud went to California with Whiteside Construction, and I stayed with my folks in Mitchell, where Daddy was still teaching. In October, I took the bus to Watsonville, California, to be with Bud. He had rented a small place at La Selva Beach, located on the coast between Santa Cruz and Watsonville. At that time, this was definitely an upper-class residential area of wide, palm-lined streets and stucco houses that exuded an air of money. The town sat on a bluff overlooking Manresa Beach and the ocean beyond it. To the east of town, the bluff dropped into a ravine, through which ran the San Andreas Road. We lived in a beach house, out of sight of La Selva Beach itself, though within hearing of the ocean. The house was of board-and-batten construction—vertical boards with narrow slats covering the cracks, stained brown, and set against the steep slope of the ravine. It had two tiny bedrooms, a bath, and a large living/dining area with a tiny, galley-style cooking area and a brick fireplace for heat. In winter, the floors were cold, as the house was open and not insulated underneath.

I liked it there. This was the first real home of my

own. I polished, scrubbed, sewed new curtains, and taught myself to knit, making a white wool baby afghan that I eventually used for both Gerry and Deidre. And I walked the beach. I was happy. I schemed and contrived Christmas presents of foam-stuffed, yarn-covered dogs and doll clothes with tiny fastenings and minute frills that we delivered back to Oregon for the Christmas holiday. When we returned to California, Lady, who had remained with my parents, went with us. On the return trip, I also acquired a beige-and-white stuffed pup that joined the black-and-white, shaggy stuffed dog on the bed.

Because Lady had to be tied so that she would not roam, I took her—or rather she dragged me—to the beach almost every day. There I would loose her from the leash and she would race among the seagulls to watch them scatter. Though they always flew away, squawking their protests, they would return to settle on the sand once she moved on. Soon they learned that she only meant to play, never to catch or harm them. Sometimes she would chase the waves as they retreated from the shore. Then she would race back as the waves returned, threatening her dancing white feet with their cold froth.

In January 1962, Bud's dad came from Northport, Washington, to stay with us and work with Bud for Whiteside. He stayed on with the company after the job was finished and we returned to Oregon. He followed

Whiteside Construction to Colorado, where he made his home from that time until his death in 1993. Bud's mother remained in Northport, but later moved to Klamath Falls to be near Carol Lee.

While we were living in California, an enormous oak limb fell onto the Ghia, crushing the top. Insurance covered the damage, and once repairs were complete, we had the car repainted. The original black paint, though perfect for the sporty car, created more heat under the sun; therefore, we selected a metallic San Marino Turquoise with a white top. The inside temperature dropped at least twenty degrees. We enjoyed the Ghia as long as we had it. Not only was it fun to drive, it was also comfortable.

In March of 1962, I took a part-time job as library page at the Watsonville City Library. I shelved books and in the process found ones that I had not read. Then I typed cards. The work was not demanding, but it provided activity to help fill empty time. About this same time, we acquired Koki, a silver poodle. I had never liked poodles because of their high-pitched yappy barks. Friends, however, had a cocker spaniel/poodle mixed breed that was delightful. Bud finally persuaded me to look at some puppies that were of registered stock but without papers. Koki was not my first choice; he was just too timid. I wanted his littermate, known as Piranha because he would bite anyone not of his immediate family. I tried very hard with him, but he nipped me. We settled for Koki, so timid that he would hide under the gas range in the kitchen whenever he heard a loud voice. We almost had to baby-talk him, as normal voices seemed to scold him. He never did get over his timidity completely, but he did improve. Lady treated him like a new toy, pinning him under one paw when she was tired of playing with him.

The job with Whiteside Construction ended, but Bud took temporary work before we returned to Oregon. We moved to new quarters—camping really. A man who had worked with Bud offered him and his dad a deal to remodel a cabin on his chicken farm. We could use it free of rent while the work was in progress. His wife, a Japanese woman named Misao, was a delightful companion during our brief stay there. She taught me how to take miniature mussel shells, cover them with scrap fabric, and with silk twist and a pin, create a lapel ornament. Somehow, plans or money did not work out as projected, and Bud decided to return to Oregon to seek work. We were back in Kimberly by late April.

Steady work in the construction field always seemed difficult for Bud to find, especially in central and eastern Oregon. Finally, in June we went job hunting in Portland, where we stayed with Ruth for a week. After culling the newspaper, I borrowed a dress from Ruth, interviewed and was accepted for a general office job with P & C Tool Company in Milwaukie, Oregon. At first, my duties were routinely clerical, but eventually,

I was given the responsibility for managing the sales-incentive program. As I had steady work, we rented a two-room upstairs apartment in a house on Boyd Street in the Ardenwald district of Milwaukie. This house was at the end of a street abutting onto the railroad. Little more than a tall hedge and the railroad right-of-way separated us from the noise of passing trains. At first, I had trouble adjusting to the racket, but eventually I became accustomed enough to the rhythmic rumble that I seldom heard it. Too, the location was within walking distance of my work, albeit a long walk, especially during rainy weather. Bud worked for a short time in the Milwaukie area, but within six months he was again in central Oregon where he had joined the carpenters' union. Too much of the time, he worked away from home, either there or elsewhere out-of-town.

We grew tired of renting and began house hunting. Following the Columbus Day storm in October of 1962, we located a small house in the Oak Grove area south of Milwaukie and moved in during Thanksgiving weekend. Now that we had our home in Oak Grove, we brought Lady from Kimberly. She once thought a neighbor's boxer was threatening me. Even though tied to the bumper of the Volkswagen bus (acquired when the Karmen Ghia failed), she lunged hard enough to break the nylon parachute cord and flew past me to launch an attack at the boxer's throat. It took both men to forcibly separate the two dogs, but Lady broke free a second time, attacking the boxer with a snarl and her lips rolled back away from her fangs. She did not go for the throat; instead, she slashed and ripped at a dead run. Her calculated attack laid the boxer's chest open. Bud and the owner took the boxer to a vet, and she survived. The neighbor never brought her back over again.

The house had two small bedrooms and had been damaged during the major storm of that year when an oak tree blew down across one corner of the living room. Except for the back porch, the rest of the house was sound. Over the next year, we repaired the roof damage, cleared the blackberry brambles back to the property perimeters, pruned shrubs, and mowed what seemed like acres of grass. Bud put on new siding and a porch rail, replaced the floor on the back porch, and built a workshop at the rear of the garage. We also began to furnish the house, as we had nothing at all when we purchased it. With only an old electric range in the kitchen, we needed everything. At Bee Salvage Company, we found an orange Naugahyde couch, which was basically four screw-in legs, a bench seat, and a detachable backboard. At a local auction, we found a small wooden table and matching chairs. Somewhere, we came up with a mattress and springs that we used on the floor until we could purchase an unfinished bookcase headboard and a frame for the mattress. Because we did not have a refrigerator, I set food on a table on the back porch, and as the weather was cold, I managed nicely without refrigeration. By the time warm weather returned, we had found a new but slightly damaged Marquette refrigerator with a cross-top freezer. An oil stove that had come with the house stood in the living room. I added a small portable television, a braided oval rug, and two wicker porch chairs. Bud redid one wall with knotty-cedar paneling, into which he built a bookcase for me. It was all quite simple, but it was home.

Outside, as we cleared the jungle of blackberry brambles, I found shrubs that had grown wild. By the time we finished, I could see the care that someone had originally taken when planning the yard. I found a tulip tree, several forsythia shrubs that blossomed yellow each spring, camellias, azaleas, and several roses. Pruning improved all of these. I had long-stemmed pink roses with blooms four and five inches in diameter.

When we moved into this house, we had Lady, Koki, and a parakeet. It was not long before we acquired a Siamese cat named Annabelle from the Portland Humane Society where she had been placed for adoption. She was a mature cat of seven and had been well loved, but her owners were away from home so much that they decided to give her away. At first, she would not eat. I tried everything—dry food, canned tuna, milk—nothing worked. I offered it to her cold and then warmed. She still would not eat. In desperation, I phoned the humane society. Normally, they would not give out names of pet donors, but this time someone bent the rules. I phoned Annabelle's previous owner, and she and her husband came to visit. They were an elderly couple and had raised Annabelle and one litter of her kittens. They even brought a picture of the litter of kittens. Even with their feeding instructions and visits, it took a long time for her to accept us and become our cat.

We worked hard to make a home in Oak Grove, but ultimately, it took more than we were ready to give. Bud's work took him out of town too much, and I was alone too much. When I tried to tell him how I felt, he did not understand

In September of 1963, I quit my job with P & C Tool Company. We sold the house and most of the furnishings, and moved back to Kimberly with my folks. We thought we had planned our move carefully, but the man who held the contract on our house would not allow us to sell, even though we had a buyer. He said he would allow us to miss a couple of payments so we could get back on our feet, but by Christmas, Bud was again unemployed, our vehicle wouldn't run, and there was no money with which to pay the house payments and the improvement loan for the much-needed siding on the house. Now the owner demanded full payment on the contract, and we could not pay. We declared bankruptcy; he sold the house to the buyer we had worked with; and we were back to square one—living in a strained situation with my parents and not at all sure that we could make it together.

The months that followed were not easy. During the summer and fall, Bud had short jobs in Canyon City and Burns. I camped out with him in an old two-room shack situated with a spring and an outhouse on the hillside above the road between John Day and Canyon City. We had a mattress on the floor, the kerosene stove that Mother had cooked over in the tent-house, a bushel basket of kitchen necessities, and spring water running by gravity flow onto a burlap-covered cupboard to keep food cool. I heated water in Mom's old teakettle. When Bud went to the job in Burns, he rented a motel room.

We wintered at Kimberly, and in March he took a job with Stinchfield in Condon. We settled into a duplex that was impossible to keep warm. Electric heat did very little to keep away the icy wind that found its way around every window and door. When I would wash clothes and hang them on the clothesline, they froze stiff as boards before I had the pins secured. A month of this, and I was looking for something else. I found a house that was completely furnished but not occupied. An elderly couple had lived there until both had to enter a rest home. Eventually, I convinced their daughter to rent the house to me, thus beginning one of the happiest times of my life. I cooked, baked, cleaned, worked in the yard, and started oil painting again. I painted *Mont Blanc* and *Mare with a Foal* while living there. I sold the first painting to a neighbor ten years later, and the second eventually found a home with Carol Lee and Bill Hood.

The house was small but well built and cozy. It came complete with French doors, an upright piano, a dining room with a curved-glass china cabinet, real carpet, overstuffed chairs, footstools, and a fireplace. The kitchen was small but efficient and opened onto steps leading down to the back door and to the basement where Bud installed the washer and dryer next to a large double laundry sink.

Once spring weather turned warm, I raked winter's debris from the yard and began cleaning flowerbeds where I found sprouting bulbs that became a carpet of yellow, purple, and white crocus framing the house. I also began to hang my laundry on the line to take advantage of the sunshine and fresh air. One of those trips to the clothesline cost Annabelle the Siamese the tip of her tail when she slipped out to follow me. The storm door closed sharply with its strong spring closure, and the edge of the door pinched the very tip of her tail. Damage to the tailbones left her with a permanent kink.

After making the house mine, I joined a painting group where I learned to paint fluffy summer clouds. I even looked for work. As Condon is a small town in wheat country, I was within walking distance of every place I needed or wanted to go. I shopped for groceries at the local market, and they delivered the groceries to my front step. The butcher shop was small, but the meat was excellent. I found good pot roasts, ground beef, and oxtail for stew at twenty-nine cents a pound.

At this shop, I was also able to get bones for Lady and Koki.

Although I was happy here, Bud was not satisfied with his job. He felt he was not earning enough to have to take the nonsense that came with the job. We moved again. We traded the Ghia and its mechanical problems for a used blue pickup that got me and what things we had back to Kimberly before Bud left to look for work in Bend. Through the carpenters' union, he got work on two short jobs and finally one at Kah-nee-ta and then Warm Springs. For a while, he slept in the back of the pickup or rented a motel room.

About this time, Uncle Ray died in McMinnville, and Dad had to settle his estate, which included an old twenty-six-foot trailer house similar to the one that we had lived in when Dad taught at Izee. Dad needed to move the trailer to Kimberly but had no vehicle with which to tow it. Bud traded our old blue pickup, which was not trustworthy for towing, for a bright red Ford half-ton that could do the job. Then on a weekend, we made the trip with Dad to move the trailer. After that, we went into debt again to purchase a fifteen-foot Nomad travel trailer for ourselves. This let me spend time with Bud. At first, we parked it at a campground beside the Deschutes River at Warm Springs. The late spring weather was warm, so this was like camping out. I spent my days with Koki and Mitzi, the black poodle puppy that we had gotten to give him companionship.

Lady and Annabelle were still at Kimberly with Mother. In fact, Annabelle had attached herself to my youngest sister, and when Georgia married in 1967, Annabelle went with her to Ohio.

Late in June 1964, the unexpected happened. Bud was in the Bend, Oregon unemployment office (between jobs), and while I waited for him, I visited with the secretary. She told me of a job opening available if I wished to apply. The only catch was that the interview had to be within the hour. I was dressed in white shorts and a blouse and was wearing flip-flops on my feet— definitely not a professional office look, even though I was clean and neat. I decided to chance it anyway and went for an interview. The job was as general office help for Jim Arntz Real Estate, located out on Greenwood Avenue, east of downtown Bend. Mr. Arntz said he would let me know that afternoon. I got the job but had only a week—until July 5—to get ready.

We found a place to park the trailer in an older park out beyond the underpass on South Third. If Bud was gone with the pickup, I walked about two miles to work. I walked most of the time. Before the summer was over, I had applied to and been accepted as a student at Central Oregon College, now located on its brand-new campus, where I began night classes. Thus began what some people might consider a nightmare existence. I worked from nine to five as a secretary and attended college classes from seven to ten each night.

Bud was either out of town on a job, on unemployment, or working at Truax, a nearby gas station. He even tried taking forestry courses but decided that he did not have sufficient time to work, study, and attend classes.

While taking an introduction to literature course, I received my first real experience with writing. The instructor had taught high school for twelve years and after our class submitted our first papers, he returned them and told us that we did not know how to write. We were to rewrite and resubmit until he was satisfied. I usually wrote fifteen hundred words for every five hundred that I had to turn in, so believe you me, I was learning to cut out the deadwood. Then I would have to rewrite the piece, often not knowing just why I was cutting, adding, or changing. Somehow, the process worked, and I began to develop a cleaner style of writing.

At some point, we moved the trailer to a park just north of the underpass, which although closer, still put me quite a distance from work. We left Lady with Mother and Dad, as we were living in a fifteen-foot travel trailer, located in a trailer park. With both of us gone all day, it was no place for her. She was a large dog and needed space to run. As cold weather approached, however, she began seeking out the sunshine and warmth of the highway in front of the service station at Kimberly. For her own security, we had to find another home for her. Finally, we connected with a family who had a farm near Bend. The young couple had a little boy, and the grandfather lived with them. I felt this was the best we could do for her. The last time I saw Lady, she sat in the kitchen patiently waiting for the little boy to share a bowl of Cheerios bite-for-bite with her.

We bought another poodle to replace Mitzi, who went to another home. Her personality and mine had always clashed. Princee, a champagne-colored female, was as placid in disposition as Koki was nervous. Between the two of them, we had new puppies every six months, regardless of my efforts to keep the two dogs apart. Even putting her in "panties" did not help. On the positive side, these puppies paid for all of my college textbooks. Finally, I was able to afford $400 for a used Volkswagen, even though the bank insisted on a cosigner. My boss signed for me. This was an early model that had a floor switch activating the reserve gallon of gasoline if I ran out of fuel. As I could go at least a week on one gallon of gas, I found myself stranded a number of times because I had turned the switch but had forgotten to fill the tank before it completely hit empty. Eventually, Bud convinced me to let him trade this car on a Datsun Fairlady, a sports car with a ragtop. We both enjoyed the Fairlady, but without an insulated top, she definitely was not a cold-weather car.

By February 1966, I told Bud we had to have something else to live in. The poodles spent more time in the little trailer than we did, and when two of us were in it at the same time, there was no room to spare. After looking around, we settled on a ten-by-fifty-five-foot Kit Fairview—a mansion compared to the Nomad, although in reality it had no more than five hundred square feet of living space. This home served us well for almost ten years.

By the time graduation arrived for me in June 1966, our lives were a mess. We were two people sharing a residence, but neither seemed to care about the other any more. I did not know what Bud was doing with his time, and he never asked about mine. In retrospect, I think that my school interests opened up a way of life for me from which Bud felt excluded. I was growing intellectually, thriving in the academic atmosphere, and learning to think for myself and to write. He was not interested and closed me out completely. I think we both turned to others for companionship, and perhaps even for affection.

At some point that summer, I could no longer tolerate the aloneness and finally asked for a divorce. Our communications were so poor that I did not feel I could even talk to him. Instead, I went to a lawyer for advice. Of course, he would do nothing until I talked to Bud. As we were visiting at Kimberly, Bud would not even talk. He asked me to return to Bend with him, and for some reason, I did. Perhaps I realized how one-sided my decision really was. We talked all the way home, as we should have talked earlier, and as a result, we tried to work things out. We even talked about starting a family—a real first. Whenever the subject of babies had come up before, Bud had emphatically said no. At one point, he had gone so far as to say that I could have a baby or him, but not both. End of subject.

Although I did not realize it at the time, our difficulties were the culmination of a period of growth. We were both young at the time of our marriage, and although we were comparatively mature for our generation, we still had to develop as individuals and as adults. Conflicts were inevitable. No man lives isolated from women other than his mate; likewise, his mate is exposed to the lure of other males. The situation of me working outside the home, and Bud working most frequently out of town, only enhanced the possibility that chance encounters might lead to meaningful relationships.

During the first seven years of our marriage, there were both acknowledged and unspoken encounters for both of us. Sometimes we could share these and grow in our commitment to each other. At other times, there were secrets to be hidden, either because we felt the guilt of betrayal or because one did not want to hurt the other. We were growing up.

I fell out of love—that is, reality crushed my romantic ideals under its heel. It is traumatic to wed the preacher's son and then be bedded by a GI. Naïveté and youth cloaked much ignorance, yet acceptance and understanding along with buckets of tears eventually nurtured emotional strength. I learned that love is more than moonlight and tender caresses. Love is wanting and giving, taking and sharing, hurting, healing, security, loneliness, and at last, letting go. Love does not grow where it is smothered under demands. Love needs the freedom of choice. We must make comparisons before we can choose to share. Then, perhaps, a real love begins.

Love is...

Cold feet in the hollow of my back,
Warm arms around me when I wake,
A glowing fire on a chilly night,
A glass of garnet-colored wine.

You, pounding nails, creating buildings
While I read;
You, digging bottles, hunting elk, waiting
While I learn to teach, searching.

Two people climbing stairs,
Sharing, giving of each to the other,
Knowing without asking,
Living for another, but first for self.

Chapter 6: Hearth Fires

By 1966, I believe Bud and I had come to the point that we dared to release each other to grow in our own individual ways. At least we were easy with each other. Yes, hurts lay beneath the surface, and it would not take much to tear the fragile scabs that were growing on old wounds. We had hurt each other deeply, yet our very essences stretched tentative fingers outward to each other, trying to regain and strengthen those ties that still held.

My graduation from Central Oregon College brought new decisions. I had applied to the University of Oregon and to Eastern Oregon College. A move to Eugene would mean continued rent for trailer space, and it would put us back in the Willamette Valley climate. Neither of us particularly desired that. On the other hand, school at La Grande would enable us to live in Union, where my folks had purchased property, and we liked the small town. As Dad had two extra lots that would take the mobile home that we had purchased, I selected the smaller school, and we moved to Union where we remained until the spring of 1968. Georgia, my youngest sister, had already spent one year there living in the dorm. Now, she and I set up housekeeping in Uncle Ray's old trailer that Dad had moved onto the corner lot. Bud was to move with our mobile home in late October. Mother and Dad offered to give us two of the four lots, but we refused their offer of the gift. Later, Bud agreed to accept the two lots in exchange for his work in framing a cabana addition for their trailer. Our lots had originally been pasture, but the grass was good, and there were two old Black Republican cherry trees. The old chicken house, when cleaned, made a good storage shed.

After moving the mobile home to Union, Bud worked hard to complete the framing for the cabana. He had told Dad that he did not want to work on it during elk season, but Dad kept pushing to get it done. Then, when Bud went hunting, Dad would do something or get someone else to help him on the project. Quite often, the dimensions or quality of the work did not fit with what Bud had started. This caused problems because Bud could not start working where he had left off without reworking or compensating for the added project. Eventually, however, the structure was completed.

While I attended classes at Eastern Oregon, Bud worked for Gateway Auto as a detail man. I did not attempt to work during my last two years of school, as I was carrying a heavy academic schedule that required hours of reading each night. As a night student at Central Oregon, I had missed courses that Eastern now required me to make up. At one point I was enrolled in both English history and English novel classes, and I was reading over a thousand pages a week. I often sat reading with Jolie, one of the puppies, curled on my lap. Rarely did I ever have sufficient time to really study in-depth or read material a second time. Somehow, I learned to grasp the essentials and keep moving forward.

At first, I selected education as a major area of study, but after two sessions in a general education class, I knew that would be a waste of my time. I switched to a major in English, but needing other courses to fill out my program, I signed up for English history with Mary Davidson, who made England and her people come alive for me.

During that time, I really learned how to perform in the academic world although the class load curtailed other interests. I sold Princee and Jolie, the teacup sized puppy that I had kept, because I had no time to care for more puppies. In the English department, I had the help of Dr. Loso and Dr. Clarke. Dr. Loso was considered a tough professor, and it took me an entire year in one course to achieve an A from her. She also demanded perfect spelling on term papers. I rewrote one paper three times before I spelled *loneliness* correctly. Finally, I was able to achieve A's in all of the classes that I took from her. These were English literature and poetry classes, so I had an in-depth background in at least one area. Dr. Clarke, much less demanding as a teacher, taught American literature and linguistics. I learned more from him as an advisor than I did as a teacher. One time, he was talking about maturity as it related to a character in an American novel. He told me: "We can consider ourselves mature when we are able to accept our parents as we would strangers without making demands of them just because they are related to us." This concept helped me more than once after that.

It took me a long time before I was able to do this in my life. Until I learned to accept Mother and ignore the way she kept house, nagged, or slept away her time, I was constantly uptight because I felt she should change. Once the situation was in perspective and I could admit that I could not change her, I was able to enjoy her good points. It was either that or do something myself to change the aspects that I did not like, and I refused to do her housekeeping as well as keep up my own home.

During these last two years of school, I picked up more French and a smattering of German, along with one class in drawing. Other than that, literature and history dominated my courses. I had taken one year of biology to fulfill my science requirement and took no math classes at all. In March of 1968, I finished a degree in English with honors. As a transfer student, I was not in the honors program; thus, the *Summa cum laude* honor was totally unexpected.

Before I completed my courses, I had listened to the armed-forces recruiters who made career options, especially for advanced education, seem a possibility for me. At that time, the navy had a more attractive program for women than the army offered, although the army program was not really a bad choice. At first, Bud thought I was joking, but when we looked at the offerings, he too began to see a possible chance for us to travel and do some of the things we could not do any other way.

As I still had no career skills, even though I had a college education, I was considering the armed services as a means to gain further education as well as travel. I completed the paperwork for the navy, only to have them tell me that programs were no longer open to married women. So I tried the army. They had no such problem. By my June graduation, I had gone through the typical army physical where I felt like a piece of merchandise going through quality control. I was not given even a paper gown, only a small—I mean very small—terry towel. Even so, I survived and passed the required tests. The only thing left was to wait for induction and orders to send me to Alabama for basic training.

Meanwhile, Bud had headed for the Portland area to seek work, as there was nothing available in the La Grande area. For a brief time, he arranged to stay with his aunt and uncle, Ruby and Al Adams, who lived near Hillsboro. Moving back to Portland was not what we had planned to do, but it seemed to be where the jobs were located.

I visited him there and went to the recruiting office in Portland to ask about my status. The information I received there contradicted what I had heard from the Boise officers. I then went to Klamath Falls to visit Bud's sister. While there, I received a call from the Boise headquarters and was royally chewed out for going to the Portland office. As I recall, the Boise office then more or less confirmed what I had heard in Portland: I would not be able to have the mobile home moved, and Bud would not have the same dependent privileges that I had had when he was a member of the air force. That altered my plans considerably. I was already married and had a life without the military. Because I wanted more not less, a career in an organization prejudiced against women just did not fit my idea of what I wanted from life. Ultimately, I told my recruiter that my marriage had preceded my application to the army, that I wasn't single, and as I had not yet signed away my life, I wasn't interested. End of subject.

Now what? I joined Bud in Portland and began job hunting. By August of 1968, I was working in the office of Ness Produce Company, a food distributor located just off Burnside and Second, on the east side of the river. Bud worked in construction wherever the union sent him, but he had time to deer hunt one weekend in Kinzua where Ruth and her family lived. We returned to Portland with Sheba, a chocolate-point Siamese cat who had been surviving in the local dump.

We had moved the mobile home into a park on Jenkins Road in Beaverton, not far from the airport that later was developed into a suburban shopping mall. We had given up on the idea of children, and I had begun to think that I was unable to have any. Then one day during the winter, nothing seemed to go right at work, and I fell apart over some problem that I would normally have taken in stride. When Lydia, a coworker, asked me what was wrong, I began to cry. She said, "I've been watching you. I think you are pregnant." I was astonished, as this was the farthest thought from my mind. She had had eight children of her own, though, so I went to see a doctor who confirmed her diagnosis.

Nothing really changed right then except I felt sick every morning. I kept dry saltine crackers on the bedside table and ate one or two before getting up. That helped. After that, I could usually manage to keep down a banana that I would eat while driving to work. By my ten o'clock coffee break, I was ready for something else, usually a slice of ham with dry toast at a diner not far from work.

I liked Dr. Callas, my obstetrician, but I did not want to have a baby at Good Samaritan Hospital. It was just too big. Eventually, I arranged to return to Dr. Rose and Grand Ronde Hospital in La Grande. Sometime in the spring, Bud and I went to watch the Spanish Riding Academy perform at the Coliseum. While walking down the stairs afterward, I felt small pains. A show of blood followed, though nothing seemed to be wrong. The baby, whom we called Thumper, was due in late September. That meant I could work until August, which I did with no problems other than normal discomfort and feeling clumsy. Bud delivered me to my folks in Union but then returned to his carpentry work. Then I waited. As my time came and went, I picked and canned apricots, made baby quilts with Mother, and helped Dad hang sheetrock on the ceiling of the added-on living room. Still nothing.

Thumper was overdue. I was having steady contractions that, though mild, never went away. Dr. Rose finally decided to use castor oil to induce true labor. After I phoned Bud and checked in at the hospital, Dr. Rose "broke the waters," hoping that would speed up the delivery, but I still was not dilating sufficiently. I spent fifty-two long, uncomfortable hours before Gerald Frederick was born on October 13, 1969, a very snowy day. Bud had left his work in Washington when I called him, and was at the hospital when Gerry was born.

I stayed with my folks until Dr. Rose gave Gerry a two-week checkup. Then Bud and I returned home to Portland. We then headed for Reno, Nevada, where we visited with our friends Jim and Geri Hall, the first stop of a brief vacation to show off the new baby. Gerry cried more than usual and seemed to be in pain. At night, he was quiet only as long as someone paced the floor with him. When we were driving to Lake Tahoe, he began screaming incessantly as we gained in altitude. We turned back and the lower elevation helped; I never did see Lake Tahoe.

On the return trip to Portland, we stopped by Klamath Falls to introduce Gerry to Bud's mother and his sister Carol. We also stopped in Bend for a few minutes with the Budke family. Back at home, Bud was out of work and Gerry was not doing well; he had trouble nursing. I took him to Kaiser for his six-week checkup, and the doctor wanted to send him to the children's hospital. He explained to us that there were major problems with Gerry's heart that would require specialists and surgery. Gerry died November 29, 1969, following surgery. His existence could not mend a flawed relationship, and his death said, "It's over. Move on." But I could not hear. My life was not the same after that.

**

Yellow leaves on thin
Black arms whimper in sunlight:
Northern wind blows cold

**

Chapter 7: An Ending

Over ten years later I finally faced Gerry's death, and during a writing course at Southern Oregon State College I dealt with my pain by using fiction to write about his death—the short story that follows.

Sometimes a Cold Wind...

Something was wrong. The stethoscope moved across the tiny chest, first on one side and then on the other, then around to the back, again and again. The doctor's face, partially cloaked by a grey-streaked black beard, told her nothing—and yet told all.

"I need x-rays." He looked up at her as he removed the stethoscope from his ears. "You can dress the baby now. I'll talk to you in my office."

Jenny repinned Jeremy's diaper and pulled the tiny shirt over his head. "Shh. That's all right," she crooned as he began to cry. She cuddled him close for a moment, but his wails continued. Hurriedly, she dressed him in his blue terry sleeper, swaddled him in a soft flannel blanket, and then held him against her shoulder.

"I must phone Sam," she told herself as she returned to the waiting room. Bouncing the baby gently, she crossed to the receptionist. "May I use your phone? Dr.

Peters wants a conference"—her fear made her voice break—"and I want to contact my husband."

"Do you have the number?" asked the dark-haired girl as she turned to the phone.

"No, but he'll be across the street at Jafco. Please— ask them to page him."

The girl dialed, made the request, and handed the phone to Jenny. As she waited, fighting back tears and trying hard to regain control, she continued to jiggle the baby who was still fussing, though not as loudly as before.

"Hello…" Sam's voice already held a note of alarm.

"Sam, it's Jenny. The doctor wants a conference about Jeremy. Will you…come…" Her voice broke again.

"I'll be right there!" The receiver clicked sharply in her ear.

"Thank you," she said, handing the receiver to the receptionist. Turning, she walked across the room, sat down, and began to rock her baby, holding him as if he were the most fragile and precious thing in her world. She was twenty-seven, but a ray of afternoon sunlight falling on her bent head revealed a touch of silver in her dark hair. It also brought out a hint of auburn that picked up the color in her cheeks and set off her large grey-green eyes, now darkened by stress.

The front doors slid open, and she looked up, tilting her head slightly to one side. A tall, darkly tanned man strode quickly to where she was sitting. His brows arched above blue eyes; a beard and well-trimmed sideburns framed his lean face and blended into grey-blond hair that fell thinly across a high forehead.

"What's wrong?" Sam sat down beside her.

"I don't know," she whispered, "but he kept listening and listening to Jerry's heart. He did it over and over."

Sam reached out with a strong, slender hand, took Jenny's, and gripped it until her knuckles turned white, a mute acknowledgment of concern.

At that moment, a middle-aged, motherly looking nurse stepped into the room on noiseless feet. "Mrs. Scott?" She swept her look across the six or so women, including Jenny, who were waiting. Startled, Jenny looked up.

"Yes?"

"Come this way, please. Doctor will see you now." She turned and hurried down a long sunlit corridor. Without speaking, Sam and Jenny followed. The nurse opened a dark, paneled door that led into a large corner office with windows on two walls. "In here, please. Doctor will be with you shortly." She left, closing the door behind her.

Jenny stood just inside the room, blinking against the

play of sunlight on the white-walled building across the way. Then afraid to speak, she moved toward an armchair turned partially away from the windows. Resting her left arm on the chair arm, she folded the blankets away from Jeremy's face. He was sleeping at last, but his breath rasped through his half-open mouth. They waited, the three of them—two avoiding the questions that might voice the uncertain future of the third.

"I'm Dr. Peters." The voice came from the doorway behind the large walnut desk. The doctor stepped around his desk, hand extended toward Sam.

"Sam Scott." Sam gripped the doctor's hand in a firm shake. When both men had taken their chairs, the doctor continued.

"That's a very sick boy you have there." Jenny felt her heart sink. "As I told your wife earlier," he continued, speaking directly to Sam, "I need x-rays. I need these before I can determine just how sick the baby is. In fact, I want you to admit him to Children's Hospital today."

With clenched fists and words that came with tremendous effort, Sam forced out the question. "Just what is the problem, Doctor?"

"His heart."

Tears filled Jenny's eyes and spilled over, spreading

mascara-streaked rivulets down her cheeks. Sam's breathing was fast and shallow.

"In most cases like this," Dr. Peters went on, "there's an excellent chance for surgery. You see, the problem is a vein that connects the heart and lungs prior to birth. Usually it disappears. When it does not, too much blood in the lung area causes breathing difficulty and respiratory congestion. Surgeons can now tie this vein off with Teflon. Then, usually when the child is two years old, open-heart surgery is performed to repair any other damage, such as the holes that are normally present in these cases that cause blood to flow between the chambers between heartbeats. Jeremy has a chance because we've caught the problem now, and he is still holding his weight."

Jenny looked at her sleeping son. *So tiny! Only eight pounds. That's six ounces less than when he was born six weeks ago!*

"I recommend immediate catheterization to determine the extent of damage," the gentle voice of the doctor continued. "It's risky, to say the least, but it's necessary."

Sam looked at Jenny, frustration and anger almost glazing his eyes. "Honey…" A sob caught in his throat, and he stopped. Mutely she met his look. *I know…*the slate grey eyes, wet with tears, said eloquently. Taking a deep breath and turning to face the doctor, Sam plunged in.

"What are his chances?"

"With catheterization, pretty good, but without? I just don't know."

"We have to give him that chance," Jenny spoke, her voice choking with tears.

Sam nodded. "What do we do now?"

"I've already phoned the hospital. I want you to take him there immediately." The doctor then gave Sam directions to Children's Hospital, a branch of University Medical School, but Jenny heard only the murmur of their voices.

*Risky chance...*the words kept repeating inside her head and blocked out all else until Sam touched her on the shoulder.

"Let's go, honey."

Thirty minutes later, they entered the glass-fronted building where doctors—sometimes—wrought miracles.

"I'm Sam Scott." They stepped up to the reception desk. "Dr. Peters just phoned to admit our son Jeremy."

"Oh yes," the woman at the desk replied. "Dr. Lathrop is expecting you. He's on the fourth floor. Check with the desk there." As they turned away, she added, "Stop back here on your way out. There are some forms we need to complete."

For Sam, an afternoon of carefree shopping had become a long, frustrating wait. For Jenny, the day turned into a nightmare of green-gowned doctors, crowded cubicles, chilly, bleak rooms, and tests and tests and more tests. Finally, after removing a lead apron that had seemed to be crushing her into the tiled floor as she held Jeremy immobile for one last x-ray, she was able to return to Sam.

She looks beat, he thought, as he reached to take the crying baby from her. "All finished?"

Jenny nodded, "Except for taking him to the nursery. It's down there." She gestured to a hall that disappeared to their left. She gathered her purse, Jeremy's bag, and the hand-knit white afghan that she had left on the chair beside Sam. Then she walked resolutely down the dimly lit corridor and into the nursery, where a nurse met them.

"We'll put Jeremy in here." The grey-haired woman led the way to one of two cribs in a small adjoining room. "Here, put these on him, and then you can feed him. I think he's hungry!" She smiled as she looked at the now red-faced, squalling infant. She held out a tiny gown and a disposable diaper. As Jenny took them, she felt the roughness of the sterile flannel gown. Sam watched as she changed the baby's clothing. He could do nothing to help.

"Use this to wrap him in." The nurse handed Jenny a small patchwork quilt that yielded stiffly as she tried to snuggle the baby into it.

"Can't I use his blanket?" Jenny protested, reaching for the thick, brushed-flannel one that he was used to.

"No," the nurse said firmly. "It isn't sterile and these are. Now, I'll get you some formula. Then we can put him to bed."

"I nurse him," said Jenny, beginning to unbutton her blouse.

Jeremy, tired of the hours of handling and probing, was still crying, but as Jenny shifted him to her left arm and gave him her breast, his cries decreased and became soft *unh, unh, unhs* of pleasure. Ten minutes later, he was asleep. Jenny gently placed him in the crib and kissed him good-bye before she turned to go. Sam brushed a long finger fondly over his son's pale cheek, raised the side of the crib, and followed Jenny.

Despair overcame Jenny as they drove home, two instead of three. Her empty arms ached, and tears ran unheeded down her face.

"It isn't fair," she sobbed. "Why us?"

"I don't know." Sam clenched the steering wheel, and his voice was rough. "I won't let him die!" He, too, was feeling the strain. His knuckles whitened as he whipped the car around a curve.

The next day was Tuesday—a morning filled with crisp, late-November sunshine. Sam and Jenny returned to the hospital. They had a few precious minutes with Jeremy as Jenny nursed him for the last time.

"Doctor has ordered a low-sodium formula for him," the day nurse told her. "We're to start him on it at the next feeding. Don't worry," she added, seeing the frown on Jenny's face. "Actually, it will be easier on him than nursing—less strain, Dr. Lathrop says." With that, she left the three of them alone.

Sam had brought the camera, and now he took several pictures of Jenny and Jeremy. He set the camera, and when she had finished nursing the baby, had her take a picture of him holding his son. Both of them were laughing as he held the tiny boy stretched out before him, supported by strong, tanned arms.

"I hope it's a good one. It's the last shot."

She exchanged camera for baby and began to rock him to sleep. This did not seem to take long, as his head soon drooped on her shoulder like a flower petal exhausted and battered by the rain.

The meeting that followed with Dr. Lathrop and three of his colleagues in an empty room with a bed but no chairs, held only one sentence for Jenny: "With catheterization, his chances are fifty/fifty; without, he won't live thirty days."

The words rang in her ears as she felt Sam's arm go tight around her waist.

"When?" he asked through clenched teeth.

"First thing in the morning." Dr. Lathrop smiled at them. "We've already scheduled it."

The tall, thin doctor on his right broke in, "You do realize the risk there is, don't you?"

They nodded, and Sam looked at the new speaker. "Dr. Peters explained it to us."

"This is actually more dangerous than the surgery," Dr. Lathrop continued. "If he survives this, he has an excellent chance in surgery, but there are no guarantees." He walked them to the elevator. "You should be able to see him by noon tomorrow." His voice was gentle but matter-of-fact. "We'll see you then."

"We must phone the family," Jenny commented as they crossed the asphalt parking lot. Sam nodded. They said little else, as each hurt where no words could reach.

I should have noticed sooner, thought Jenny. *He quit eating solid food while we were in Reno last week, and he couldn't keep his milk down on Monday. He just seemed to have colic, but I should have known something was wrong when he cried so much as we drove up the mountain to Lake Tahoe. It must have hurt him to breathe.*

They had not even reached the lake, she remembered, when Jeremy's cries became agonized wails of pain that had not stopped until they had turned around and descended the mountain.

Behind the wheel, Sam too, was berating himself. *Why didn't I see quicker? Jeremy was so pale, so delicate looking. Is something wrong with me? Oh God! What have I done to deserve this? He can't die. Not this way!*

At home, Jenny was able to call Sam's sister. "It's Jeremy," she said after Elizabeth answered the phone. "He's in the hospital. It's his heart."

"Oh no!" Jenny heard the shock in Elizabeth's voice. "How serious is it?"

"If he survives catheterization tomorrow, he has a chance," Jenny answered and began to cry. She handed the phone to Sam and ran sobbing to the bedroom where she threw herself on the bed and grabbed Shaggy, the black-and-white stuffed dog that Sam had gotten her shortly after they were married ten years earlier. She clenched him to her, shuddering in a paroxysm of hurt and fear.

Sam phoned his mother; then he called Jenny's folks in Union who said they would drive to Portland that night. Moral support, her father Walt had said quietly.

It was a long night as Sam held Jenny close, and they sought comfort from each other, his tears mingling with hers on the pillow.

"He's fine!" These words from Dr. Lathrop the next day gave their lives back to them.

"Can we see him?"

"Yes. You can even feed him." The doctor, still talking, walked them to the nursery. "It's a bit tricky though—we have him in an isolette with oxygen to make his breathing easier and to keep him at a stable temperature. He's all wired up, too," he added, pointing to the tubes and wires going to IVs and monitors. "We've scheduled surgery for Friday morning at nine. The sooner the better, before he starts losing weight." With that, he left them with a nurse who showed Jenny how to reach through the isolette sleeves to handle the infant.

"He doesn't like the formula," said Jenny to the nurse as Jeremy spit out the nipple for the third time.

"That's all he can have," the nurse answered flatly. "He'll get used to it when he gets hungry enough. Just let him be."

Unable to hold their son, there was little reason for them to stay, but Jenny continued to gently pat the tiny back, hoping to soothe him and lull him to sleep, but she did not succeed.

"He'll be fine when you leave." The nurse smiled as she came back into the room. "He's just used to being held. That's all."

Thursday came. Thanksgiving. They did not celebrate with turkey, but they did give thanks. Jenny wrote notes in Christmas cards that she signed, *Sam, Jenny, and Jeremy*. She visited with her mother in the kitchen. Sam and her father tried to relax with the television in the living room. They were all waiting.

Friday arrived. It was two o'clock before Sam heard the voice on the phone say, "He's in ICU, but you can see him briefly."

Jenny ran for the car, not even grabbing a coat.

"Here, put this on before you catch a cold." Sam threw her lightweight blue wool cape around her shoulders. He slid behind the steering wheel. "Ready?" He slammed his door and started the engine.

"Yes." Jenny sat bolt upright with both hands gripped together in her lap.

Twenty minutes later as they waited for the elevator, a pleasant voice paged, "Dr. Sterns to ICU, please. Dr. Sterns to ICU." The elevator arrived and slid open. They were the only passengers. Sam pushed the sublevel 1 button, and they waited.

"Put these on, please." A gowned nurse handed both Sam and Jenny sterile gowns and masks. Then she led them into the intensive care unit where machines with flickering lights and multitudinous dials seemed to come alive, surround them, hem them in. "He's heavily sedated. Asleep," the nurse said. "He won't know you. You can only stay a minute." Then she bustled off abruptly to an adjoining observation room.

Jenny hesitantly reached out to her son but drew her hand back instinctively. Bandages obscured his chest; tubes and wires were attached to his arms and legs; and tubes ran into each nostril. Somehow, he didn't seem to be hers anymore.

"You must leave now!" said a breathless voice behind them. "We'll call you when he wakes."

No call came until almost eight that night. Sam grabbed the phone at the first ring, listened, and then replaced the receiver. Mechanically, he repeated the message: "For all intents and purposes, Jeremy died at 7:27 tonight."

"No! No! No! It can't be. We've waited so long. I won't let him go! *I won't!*" Jenny fell to her knees, sobbing, out of control.

"He had the best," Sam said woodenly. "Dr. Leising from Chicago flew here to do the surgery. But it wasn't enough. He's gone."

One week later, Sam and Jenny stood hand in hand, watching as the small, white, velvet-lined casket was lowered into the ground. Soft crystals of snow fell, hiding the raw wound in the old graveyard.

"It's snowing, Sam," murmured Jenny with the first tremulous smile he had seen for some time, "just as it did the day he was born." She tossed a last red rosebud onto the white casket. Sam drew her closer, and as they turned to leave the Victorian cemetery, the wind soughed softly through the surrounding firs.

Behind the Wallowas

(An Elegy for Gerry)

An orange sun slips behind blue mountains
Turning our day crisp with cold violet light,
Painting rocks red and elderberries purple
Where they droop low between creek and road.
Scarlet leaves envy willow and birch
As they fling gold skirts on the wind, to bring back
Gerry, three winters gone (his heart they told me)
And he wasn't here for the fall.

Or the fence posts wearing top hats of white
Or the evergreens swathed in new fallen snow
Like his grave.
The grey road winds into resinous odors
And wild meadows edged by dense pine.
I see shadow-forms of dark cattle grazing;
I smell the wine odor of fallen apples and think
Of the farmwife slicing them thin or simmering
Slow for winter sauce…once a ranch, a home
With soft lights, children laughing,
strange night sounds,
And old Butch barking. Then silence.

I was curious about the old cemetery.
He had to load hay.
Across stubble of played-out alfalfa
I walk to the fence and the weeds and the trees.
Inside, thistles catch like brown claws at my legs…
Here are the graves with names unfamiliar.
I think of Union
Where his small grave lies green and clipped.

Tall grass here is burned brown by sun;
Bent grass hides rust, plot fences are down,
Names are illegible,
Moss grows plush over low headstones…
a recent date
On a clean new stone says someone knows.
Darkness falls and I listen to wind in the pines
Bringing peace though my heart catches
The faint child-note afar.

Chapter 8: Second Chances

By January of 1970, Bud was working at the Cosmopolitan Hotel on the east side of the river in Portland. Since I had quit Ness Produce before Gerry was born, I now had too much time during which to think. I had to find something to do. I applied for and received a loan that let me return to Portland State University to work toward my master's degree. (I had already taken two classes just for the fun of it.) I threw myself into books and study again as an escape from pain and grief. I selected three periods of English literature for my core studies: the beginnings to Beowulf, Middle Ages, and nineteenth century. The nineteenth century was a mistake, as it placed me in Victorian literature when I had wanted early twentieth century. Oh well. Then I had to decide whether to take a degree in English or in teaching. Because the biggest difference would be four more credits (one course), I opted for English. The way everything worked out later on, I would have been ahead to have taken the degree in teaching.

By the end of May 1970, I discovered that I was again pregnant. Between that and warm spring classrooms, I had a terrible time concentrating on some of the material. I had selected a course in advanced Chaucer, as I had enjoyed it as an undergraduate student and hoped to deepen my knowledge of this writer's body of work. I wanted to build on what Dr. Loso had given me, but this particular instructor was dull, unimaginative, and presented no challenges. I found it hard to keep my mind on Chaucer when the sun was shining and the air was warm outside. Ultimately, I daydreamed through this class on the strength of my previous study. I persevered through the summer to complete my degree requirements, finishing in August at the end of the summer term. If I learned nothing else during this time, I did learn how to use a library for research. This would help me later when I began my family history research. Finally, I finished my course work, submitted my papers, and sat for my orals in August. Even though I received that all-important piece of paper known as a "sheepskin" the following June, I had not added to my marketable job skills.

Following the end of summer term, I spent my time "building my nest" with needle and thread. I made tiny nightgowns, a bunting, small quilts and crib quilts, and I waited. At Christmas, we went back to Union for the holiday, but I stayed when Bud returned to his carpentry work in Bellingham, Washington. Thumper II was not due until the end of January 1971, but traveling was hazardous, and I wanted to be in La Grande for this second delivery.

Again, I used fiction to tell of Deidre's birth. She is very precious to me, but I needed distance—detachment—to describe the trauma and exhilaration that I felt.

A Second Chance

"I sure hope the roads aren't icy this morning," said Katherine as she looked into the bedroom where Jenny was touching up her hair.

"Why is that, Mom?" Jenny gave one last upward flip with her brush.

"Well, you know how I am about winter driving, but I am getting better about it!"

"My appointment isn't until ten thirty." Jenny turned toward her mother. "The roads should be fine by then."

"I know, honey, but there's still a chance of ice on the shady corners."

"Look! If you're going to get all bothered about it, I'll drive." Exasperation filled Jenny's voice. She hated the defensiveness and insecurity that she sensed in Katherine.

There had been ice early in December, but Sam had driven, and the trip east to Union had been uneventful. By mid-January, what snow had fallen at Christmas was gone. Last night, though, a fresh fall, not much more than a dusting, had whitened the ground with crystals that sparkled in the morning's pale sunlight.

"Really, Jenny, you don't have to get touchy about it.

I can take you in. I'll just drive slower. That's all."

"It's no problem, Mother. I feel fine. I can still fit behind the steering wheel. Besides, I'll be less nervous if I am driving."

"Well, all right, but don't you think we should leave early, just in case…" Katherine stopped, leaving her thought unspoken.

"We can, if it'll make you feel better," Jenny walked toward her mother's kitchen. "But I really don't think it's necessary."

The clinic was only a twenty-minute drive from the small town where Jenny's parents lived, but "just in case," Jenny allowed an extra fifteen minutes to make the trip. It was uneventful, and the extra wait in the doctor's office made her restless.

"Sit down and relax!" cautioned her mother. "That's the fourth time you've paced to the window and back. You're starting to act like a caged animal."

Jenny sat down again, flipped through another magazine, tossed it aside, and was on her feet again.

"What's the matter with you, Jenny?" Her mother looked up from the crocheting in her hands. "You're jumpy as a cat."

"I don't know, Mom. Maybe it's the weather. I think I'll walk to the restroom." Jenny took her time. She stopped to watch the angelfish swim lazily in their aquarium world, paused briefly to watch a sparrow search for seeds around the shrubbery outside the office window, and finally, entered the small ladies' room.

This is ridiculous, she thought as she washed her hands. *There is not a single reason I should be edgy, but I am. I don't even need to be in here. Maybe I do though. Those examinations don't need a full bladder.* As she sat, waiting, her smock jumped as the baby began to move. "Hey! Watch out! Those are my ribs." She patted the lump that had formed on her left side. The baby kicked again, this time lower down, causing a small trickle of urine to flow. There was a trace of blood on the paper afterward. *That's odd,* she thought. *I don't feel anything, not even a twinge.*

Dr. Jeff was not so nonchalant when she told him. "You're sure it was blood?"

"Yes, it was blood, but just a trace mixed with mucous," Jenny answered. "It was hardly enough to notice."

"Well, let's check and see what's going on." He buzzed for his nurse and turned to put on his gloves and warm the speculum under warm running water.

"All right, young lady, easy now," he said beginning the exam. "Hmmm," he muttered as Jenny flinched. "Is that tender, there?" He moved his fingers again.

She nodded, "A little, why?"

"That baby can come at any time." He pushed away from her and stripped off the gloves. The frown on his face drew his dark eyebrows into a line across his forehead. "When are you due?"

"The twenty-ninth." Jenny fidgeted, uncomfortable with her feet still in the metal stirrups.

"You'll never make it," he said. "You've been dilated for a month or more now, and the cervix is quite thinned and starting to soften." He sat, rubbing his chin while he thought, then noticed her discomfort. "Here, now, let's sit you up." He moved to her side and slipped an arm under her shoulders, helping her to a sitting position.

"Thank you," Jenny said, rubbing her lower back. "This is much better."

"I want you in the hospital today," he said abruptly.

"But, I'm not ready yet. I have to call Sam, write some checks, and—" She protested, but he cut her off.

"I mean it. Check in today. I'm going to be in Boise the rest of this week and all of next. That baby's not going to wait for me to get back."

"Oh. But how do you know it'll come today?" she asked quietly, no longer protesting.

"I want to induce labor. Don't worry!" he said patting

her shoulder. "We're not going to use castor oil this time. I'll give you an oral block that acts in your system just like a natural hormone. I don't think it will take long."

That afternoon, when Jenny gave her name at the reception desk, the admitting nurse looked at her. "Where have you been? Dr. Jeff's been over here every hour on the hour looking for you."

Jenny looked somewhat abashed and then laughed. "Well, he didn't give me a deadline. He said today, and I told him I'd be back this afternoon after taking care of things at home."

"Hmph" the nurse snorted as she dialed a number on her phone. "Mrs. Scott just came in, Jackie. Come get her, while I call her doctor." Without speaking to Jenny, she again dialed and waited. "Doctor? This is Madge in Admitting. Jenny Scott is here. Yes. She just came in. No, no problems. Bye." She turned to Jenny just as another nurse joined them. "Jenny, this is Jackie Gates. She'll take you to your room. Dr. Jeff will be here by the time she has you settled."

It was January 13, 1971, just fifteen months since she had walked down the same blue-carpeted hall to room 314, where she had watched the red roses bloom and fade after Jeremy's birth. Sam was still in Washington working. *He was not with me then, at the first,* she remembered, *but he was here through the worst, at the end when I really needed him.*

"Here we are," Jackie said as she entered a room and set Jenny's bag down. "I'll be back in a minute."

Jenny looked around. The room looked the same: two beds, a window looking south at the mountains, a picture on one of the green-tinted walls, a television set, and…she took a step backward to see. The number above the door was 314. It was the same room. Shaking her head in disbelief, she hung her coat in the closet and began to unpack. She had just finished when the nurse reentered the room.

"Here's a gown. Let's get you into it and then to the labor room before Dr. Jeff shows up." She moved to help Jenny with the buttons on the back of her smock.

Only minutes later, it seemed, Jenny found herself the sole occupant of the labor room and the object of the complete attention of another nurse.

"Down you go," said the older woman, whose nametag gave her name as Mabel. "This won't take long, but it's a bit unpleasant," she added as she pulled an enema setup closer to the bed. "Now, over on your left side." She helped Jenny adjust to a new position and then started the flow of water. "Tell me when you can't hold any more. I'll help you to the bathroom."

As she lay there watching the black second hand move steadily around the face of the large clock hanging on the wall beyond the foot of her bed, Jenny felt the pressure build. At first, it was just warm. Then she felt like a balloon, stretched almost to the bursting point. Soon she'd lose control. "That's enough," she told the nurse, who then disconnected the apparatus.

"Hurry!" Jenny said. "I can't hold it any longer." She sat up but needed help from the high bed.

"I'll be back in a few minutes to prep you," Mabel said once she'd seen Jenny safely into the gleaming chrome-and-white bathroom.

"Don't hurry," Jenny answered. "I learned last time that I have a delayed reaction. Five minutes back in bed, and I'll have to be in here again."

Mabel looked at her for a long minute and then walked away. She was waiting when Jenny reentered the room. Mabel walked to the sink where she fixed a pan of warm, soapy water. Then picking up a towel, a waterproof pad, and a razor, she came to Jenny's side. "Okay, now. It's time for a shave," she said, with a broad grin.

"*Not now!*" Jenny said abruptly, swinging her legs over the edge of the bed. "I told you, I'd need another trip. This is it!" When she returned to the bed, she laughed. "Last time I was here the bed had to be changed. It's awful, but that's something I can control only so long."

"At least we don't have to run you through the shower," Mabel commented as she soaped Jenny's pubic area. "You wouldn't believe some of the women that I've seen come through here. I swear," she continued between razor strokes, "some have no idea what personal cleanliness means! You, now," she said smiling at Jenny, "you're clean as a whistle."

"I did shower before my checkup this morning," Jenny commented. "But I'll probably want another when this is all over."

Mabel had just finished and tucked Jenny under a sheet, when the door opened and Dr. Jeff breezed in, bringing the smell of crisp cold winter, which the hospital had not yet smothered under antiseptics. "Where have you been?" he asked briskly, but without waiting for an answer, turned to Mabel. "Gloves, please."

"Yes, Doctor."

"Let's see how you're doing now," he said returning to Jenny. "I'll check you and break the water. That and the oral block will do the trick this time." He made his examination, checking the cervical opening with his gloved fingers. "You're still at six centimeters. That's good."

Beyond his head, Jenny could see a wall chart showing a series of circles that increased in size to indicate the cervical dilation. She still had quite a ways to go.

"This will feel like a large pin prick," he said, removing the protective wrap from an ivory-colored instrument that resembled a fourteen-inch crochet hook with a tiny blade in the hook. He inserted it gently, guiding it into position. "You'll feel warm water in a minute," he said, making the incision. "There. All done."

"I don't feel anything," said Jenny. There had been no pain and no gush of fluid.

Dr. Jeff frowned. "That's unusual. Let me take another look." He replaced the speculum, readjusted the light, and rechecked his work. "I can see where I cut the membrane, and there's a small seep of fluid oozing, but it's held back by the baby's head, which is down in position and pressing hard against the cervix." Straightening, he stripped off the gloves and stood up.

"No problem. That baby makes a good plug, that's all." He turned to Mabel and indicated a paper medicine cup sitting on the counter. "I want her to have one of these pills every half hour, without fail. I'll check back in an hour." He handed the small cup to Jenny and said, "Put this pill under your upper lip. Doesn't matter which side. Just be sure that it comes out when the next one goes in on the other side." He watched as Jenny placed the small white tablet in place. "Good girl." He patted her shoulder and left.

When he was gone, Mabel brought Katherine in. Jenny could see the weariness in her mother's face.

"Why don't you go home, Mom? You know you're tired."

"I'm fine!" her mother protested as she pulled up a chair beside the bed. "I don't mind being here. You need someone with you now."

"Mother," Jenny spoke firmly, but without anger, "I'll be all right. It will take hours yet. Labor hasn't even begun. You should go home while the roads are still good. Besides, Dad needs his supper." She waited as she watched her mother's hesitation and then added, "I can have you called when it's time. There will be plenty of time for you to come back." She looked across at Mabel with a mute appeal for support. She didn't want a repeat of the previous time when her mother had sat with her constantly, stroking her forehead, holding her hand, and talking endlessly.

Mabel ceased her busywork and crossed to Katherine. "She's right, Mrs. Graham. It will be some time yet. We can call you before she goes into delivery."

"You're sure you don't need me to stay?" Katherine asked, absently tucking the blanket around her daughter.

"Mother, it's not that I don't want you," Jenny asserted gently, sending up a silent plea for forgiveness for the lie. "It's just that you're needed at home. Really, I will have plenty of care here. I'll feel easier knowing you're getting some rest instead of sitting for hours in the waiting room."

"Don't worry about her, Mrs. Graham," said Mabel. "We'll take good care of Jenny."

"Well, all right. If you're sure. There are some things I need to do at home." Katherine leaned over, kissed Jenny, and then picked up her bag containing a partially completed baby afghan. "You will call me, won't you?" she repeated, standing in the doorway.

"Yes, Mother. I won't forget. Be careful now," Jenny admonished, trying to keep the sharpness from her voice.

Finally! Jenny reached for the magazine lying on the bed table. Then she touched the electric control, raised the head of the bed, and settled back.

"I have some things to do down the hall." Mabel interrupted just as Jenny found an interesting article on childcare. "I'll keep a check on you, but ring the buzzer if you need me before I get back."

Jenny nodded and began to read. She was about halfway into the article when a sudden contraction made her catch her breath. *It's begun,* she thought, looking at the clock and mentally noting the time. The small spasms continued as she finished the article and browsed through the rest of the magazine. At four o'clock, the fire began in her lower back and reached like great pincers until it centered in the front. She let out her breath, trying to relax and go with the pain. As it eased, Mabel came back.

"Anything yet?" she asked as she crossed the room.

"Yes. There have been regular pains for the past fifteen minutes." Jenny laid the magazine aside.

At that, Mabel put on a pair of gloves. "I'll have to check you," she said, lowering the bed and throwing the sheet aside. "Slide down this way." Just as she began to probe, another contraction began.

"That was a good one, wasn't it?" She looked at Jenny, and then as the muscles relaxed, took her measurement, and walked to the wall chart to compare her spread fingers to the circles there. She pulled off the gloves and wrote in Jenny's chart.

"You're making good progress. I'll be back."

Jenny again raised the bed. Then she reached for the bag of yarn she had brought. She pulled out a pattern book, then a hook, and white baby yarn. Her fingers moved easily through the yarn, located a loose end, and made a loop in it. She made a chain of stitches, and using it as a base, began to crochet the sole for a tiny bootee. The pains continued but began to lessen in intensity. By four thirty, they had almost stopped. That's odd, she thought. I really thought something was happening, but I suppose it's too soon.

When Dr. Jeff came in just before five, she was putting the final stitch in the sole. She looked up as the door opened.

"Well?" he asked with a quizzical look and raised eyebrows.

"I don't know," she replied. "There were some real good pains for a little while. Then everything just seemed to stop."

"Put the bed down, and I'll take a look." He rang for the nurse and put on gloves. While he waited, he glanced at Jenny's chart and Mabel's notation. "Hmmm. Looks like some progress."

When the nurse arrived, it wasn't Mabel but a young aide who was more nervous than Jenny.

"Yes, Doctor?"

"I need to check Mrs. Scott." He motioned to the lamp standing in the corner. "Move that closer, will you?"

"You're right, Jenny. There's not much going on in there right now," he said after completing the exam. He stood looking at her with a frown on his face.

"Didn't you say I was to have a block every thirty minutes?" Jenny asked as she made herself comfortable once more.

"Yes. Why?" he asked, looking at her intently. He had been her doctor since her early college days, and he knew she never asked needless questions.

"Well, the one you gave me is the only one I've had.

And it just now dissolved completely."

"Damn! Excuse me a minute," he said brusquely, as he jerked open the door and strode from the room.

The aide looked from the closed door to Jenny. "Whew! What was that about?"

"I'm not sure," said Jenny, not wanting to stir up trouble.

"Well," the girl continued, "I'm glad he wasn't mad at me!" She tidied the room and then left quietly.

The door had hardly closed behind her before it swung open again. "I want you to give Jenny one of these *right now*, and another every thirty minutes," Dr. Jeff was saying as he came in, followed by an RN. "Is that clear?"

"Yes, Doctor. One now, another to be repeated every thirty minutes."

"That's right." He watched as she gave the tablet to Jenny. "Good. You remembered," he said with approval as he saw Jenny put it under her lip on the right side. "I'll be back about six, and on site until this is over. You'll be fine now."

Again, Jenny was alone with her crocheting and her thoughts. *Sam should be getting off work about now. Wonder how long it will take him to drive here. It was a long drive before Christmas, and we almost stayed the night in Pendleton, but the coffee we stopped for helped, and Sam insisted on driving clear through. I hope he doesn't do that tonight. He has to come all the way from Seattle. That's an extra four hours of driving. He'll be tired by the time he gets home. If he stops to sleep there, maybe he'll make it here by noon tomorrow.* She sighed and let her work drop onto the bed. *I'm glad he's back to work, but I wish I could see him.* He had been with her at Christmas, but that had been three weeks earlier.

Labor pains began again as the nurse arrived to give Jenny another tablet. They continued regularly, about ten minutes apart, but other than mild discomfort did not interrupt Jenny's rhythm with the needle and yarn.

She had just finished a bowl of bouillon and begun work on the second bootee when Dr. Jeff returned.

"Still not much water," he commented as he checked her progress. "You're dilating nicely, but it'll be awhile yet." Then he turned to the nurse. "Keep up the medication, and call me as soon as…" The rest of his words were cut off by the sound of running water as he washed his hands before putting on his dark tweed jacket.

"Now, you get a nap if you can," he admonished Jenny. "I won't be far away."

"I'll try," Jenny said, as she picked up her yarn and needle. "It's hard, though. I'm too keyed up to sleep.

This baby's long overdue."

"How's that?" He cocked his head to the side. He knew he was inducing labor at least two weeks early.

"We waited nine-and-a-half months for Jeremy, and we wanted him so badly. Then we lost him, and I couldn't seem to get pregnant again." She looked at the doctor before continuing. "So, really, I've been waiting about fourteen months for Thumper II."

"I see," he nodded. "I'll do my best to see you don't wait much longer." With that, he turned to go, but added, "I mean it, Jenny. Try to get some rest."

"Yes, Doctor!" she said meekly, but they both knew she wouldn't sleep.

**

"Ohhh…" Jenny gasped, dropping the crochet hook and bootee. Her hands flattened along the cool sheets and then became tightly clenched fists. Her eyes were shut, but she forced them open to watch the clock. Ten o'clock. The burning wedge of pain across her back inexorably spread outward, encircled her, and became talons that gripped with hot needlelike claws. They held. She opened her mouth to pant with shallow breaths. Then suddenly, she felt an uncontrollable urge to push, to bear down. Sixty seconds—one whole minute. Then nothing.

She sank back against the pillow, releasing the tension of her arched back. As she drew a long, deep breath, she picked up the needlework that had fallen unheeded when the pain began. *Maybe I'll get it done.* She worked steadily and had just tied off the final stitch and clipped the yarn when the next wave of pain washed over her.

This is not the way everyone said it would be, she thought, in an attempt to ignore the tightening band around her middle. *The pains are supposed to be closer together, not further apart!* The black hands marked 10:20. She caught her breath and rang the buzzer. As the night nurse hurried in, Jenny said, "I need a bedpan— and call Dr. Jeff! *Hurry!*" As the nurse searched for a bedpan, Jenny had already thrown the blanket aside.

"What happened?" asked the nurse, helping her to sit up.

"Not much. Just steady contractions until twenty minutes ago. Since then, two whoppers. Something has changed."

The nurse waited until Jenny was resettled. The plastic-backed pad beneath Jenny was still only slightly damp, she noted. Then she quickly went to alert Dr. Jeff. She was just preparing to check Jenny when Dr. Jeff burst through the door, still struggling into his white coat.

"What's this all about, Jenny?" he asked as he

scanned the notes on her chart. Nothing there indicated any imminent rush.

"I had steady contractions until ten; then a whopper; nothing more until 10:20; then another. I felt like I had to push, and I mean *push*!"

He placed his right hand on her abdomen; there was no tightening, no contraction. He frowned. It was 10:35. If delivery was close, contractions should be regular and strong. Still…

"Gloves!" he snapped at the nurse, "and move that light a little closer."

Jenny eased herself down and drew up her knees. He had hardly inserted his fingers when suddenly they were caught in the viselike grip of a strong contraction. He placed his left hand against the bulging abdomen; this time, it was tight and hard. Definitely a strong one. Then he felt the push begin. It was as if a dam was bulging below the waterline, still intact but ready to shatter with a sudden blow from behind. When the contraction faded, he could tell that dilation was almost full.

"This is it, young lady," he said to Jenny. Turning to the nurse, he continued, "Get her ready for delivery while I change."

A gurney appeared seemingly out of nowhere. Two sets of hands helped her onto it. Someone wheeled her out and through the double swinging doors. All the faces were masked; shapeless figures draped in green moved in and out of her range of vision.

Pain was all-encompassing, steady. They had to wait. She could not move. Then quickly, the clumsy shift from gurney to table. It was rigid, hard under her tired back. Someone slipped a pillow beneath her head. Her hands gripped the cold steel of the table; it was refreshing, like ice on a hot July day. The table had hinged shelves that swung out to support her arms as a nurse began to strap her wrists down.

"Do you have to do that?" protested Jenny.

"It's safer," said the nurse. "You can't fling your arms and hurt yourself or someone else."

"I don't do that!" Jenny retorted.

"We must secure this arm, anyway," the nurse said, as she buckled the leather strap on Jenny's left arm. "I have to put an IV setup here."

"What do I need that for?" Jenny asked her.

"It's a precaution, and it saves time later, if for any reason the doctor wants you to have medication."

"That hurts!" Jenny told her emphatically, grabbing her left shoulder with her free right hand, as the refrigerated fluid made its way through her vein.

"You won't feel it very long; I just gave you a mild sedative with it."

Jenny turned her head toward the large round mirror beyond her feet. It was tilted so that she could watch the baby's birth. She floated—somehow outside herself, yet still aware of the urgent pains. She watched the nurses wrap her legs in snowy drapes; felt her feet placed in the awkward shining steel stirrups and strapped into place. All sense of time and place gave way. She withdrew and centered on the mounting pain at her core.

"All right, Jenny. I'm going to give you the local now."

That was Dr. Jeff. *Where did he come from? I didn't hear him come in.* She made herself focus on him. All she could see was green: a cap, a mask, another shapeless form seated beyond her draped legs. She felt his hands, then the sharp sting of the anesthetic and a searing jet that coursed into her left hip and burned. Instinctively, she flinched and withdrew her inner self—away from the point of the needle and the arcing arrow of fire. In reality, she had not moved at all: leather straps anchored her to steel.

Almost instantly, she felt the pains lessen. She knew when the contractions came because the drug did not mask the urge to push. She felt herself bear down against the table. A nurse, behind her head, wiped the sweat from her face, and Jenny felt the cool of wet hair against her neck.

This is work! Again she was compelled to rid herself of the burden she carried.

"Here it comes," said Dr. Jeff. "Okay, Jenny, bear down when I tell you to…" He reached for something. "Easy now. Ready? Now!" he urged her as another contraction began. "That's enough. Relax. I'm going to do the episiotomy now."

She knew when he cut through the cervical muscle, yet there was no pain—only the dull sensation of something cut.

"The head's coming now. I need a steady pressure, Jenny."

She focused, held her breath, and kept her eyes on the mirror for that first look.

"A little more now," he told her. "It's almost through."

She felt the expulsion, the sudden surge of pain that overpowered the anesthetic, and though she braced to flow with it, could not restrain a single, explosive, "Ohhh," her only cry throughout the ordeal. Then she saw her baby's head as Dr. Jeff wiped away the blood and mucous.

"Easy now, Jenny," he said, as he took a syringe and cleaned the tiny nose and throat. Then she watched him put drops into the eyes. It was a perfectly shaped head.

"Now the shoulders. This is the big one. Ready?" he asked as he felt a wave of contraction sweep through her.

She took a deep breath, remembering the agony with Jeremy at this stage. She had felt torn in half. Then as the pain centered, she clenched her fists and pushed.

Plop! Splat! It was over as the baby exploded into the rubber-apron-covered lap of the doctor. A rush of pent-up fluid followed, and Jenny lay empty, deflated, like a balloon whose air has rushed away.

She watched as Dr. Jeff grabbed the baby to keep it from sliding to the floor. Then he glanced at the clock. "Time of birth, 11:57," he announced. She saw him sever the umbilical cord and heard the not-so-tiny wail, "*Waahh! Waahh!*"

"Here's your girl, Jenny," he said, holding the baby up. "I didn't even have to swat her." He handed the baby to a waiting nurse who placed her in a readied isolette and took her to an adjoining room where she would weigh and measure the new arrival. Jenny tried to watch, but was unable to see around corners.

The double doors behind her head opened, and she heard someone say, "It's her husband on the phone, Doctor. Shall I tell him?"

"He's waited as long as I have," Jenny interrupted.

"Tell him."

Now Sam knows we're all right, she thought as she savored the experience. Floating on sedative and exhilaration, she vaguely felt the contractions begin again. Then Dr. Jeff interrupted.

"You're going to have to work again. Push." Her muscles contracted, and she bore down with the pain, forcing out the placenta.

"Good. Now to sew you up and get both of you out of here," he said, placing a bloody mass into a basin held by a nurse. As he worked with sutures, she watched Kirsten, who had been cleaned up and was back where Jenny could see her. The tiny fist was knuckled against her mouth. Her eyes opened. *They're blue like her daddy's,* Jenny thought.

My Little Girl

She peeks at me—my little girl,
Blue cornflowers amid spun gold
As skirts twirl about her dancing form.
She's my little girl.

With grubby face and muddy shoes,
She squirrels round about me
Unspent energy seething as she flits.
That's my little girl.

Deidre Louise was born January 13, 1971. We chose her first name from a book character because it was one Bud liked. Her middle name was that of her aunt Iris Louise Kloster. Although Bud was not with me during the birth, he did make the long trip safely and arrived, as I expected, the next day.

Adjustments

After the more rural atmosphere of Union, the thought of Portland and all of its hustle and bustle was unsettling. Even though we were living in Beaverton, I was not happy to return there following Deidre's birth. I really did not want to return to the Portland area. In April when Bud finished his current job, we decided to risk moving back to eastern Oregon, even though job prospects were slim to nothing and neither of us was working. Bud eventually went to work as a carpenter on the construction of the Interstate 80 (now known as I-84) overpasses near La Grande.

With the mobile home moved back to the Union lots next of Mother and Dad, I planted a weeping birch tree where I hoped it would one day shade the home we would build. I selected seeds for a flower garden, and planted my rose bushes for a rose garden. In between times, I washed diapers and watched a baby grow.

During the first part of July, the carpenters went on strike. As Bud had some time when he would not have to report in or picket, we headed for Colorado. Bud's dad had not yet seen Didi, (we called her that because she was too tiny for Deidre) and she was almost six months old. She was no longer a tiny infant, but she still fit into the bathroom washbasin for a bath at her grandpa's. She thought that was a great way to spend her time on hot afternoons.

I had looked for work, placing applications at various agencies in La Grande, but with no success. Civil service positions with the state of Oregon were rarely vacant in local offices, but I took the typing and written tests necessary to qualify for secretarial and clerical positions. Later, one interviewer told me I was overqualified for the job that he needed to fill. I took the written tests for the local law-enforcement agency and scored higher than the male applicants. Even so, only one member of a family could be hired, and as Bud was seriously trying for a position there, I withdrew my application. In the end, neither of us worked for the police department.

Finally, in August, Dr. MacArthur, superintendent of the Eastern Oregon Experiment Station at Union, phoned me for an interview. His secretary was retiring, and he needed a replacement. I was pleased—the job location was less than four blocks from the house. We seemed to hit it off, and he was not intimidated by my master's degree when I was asking for office work. My job duties included normal routines of telephone, typing, filing, and accounting; however, in addition, I learned how to read the weather instruments and make the daily weather reports for the local newspaper. Eventually, I spent much of my time with data compilation for the animal experiments and in typing the manuscripts that were submitted for publication. Before I left there, I was even working in the lab, grinding samples and making slides.

The carpenters eventually settled their contract, and Bud returned to construction work in the La Grande area. Most of what is now I-84 was under construction at this time, and the bridges and overpasses kept carpenters busy. Being on the lots next to my parents, made it convenient for my mother to care for Didi while I worked during the day. Also, I was close enough to go home for lunch and to give Didi a noon nursing, time that I enjoyed with her.

It seemed as if things were going well for us at last. We both had jobs and enjoyed where we lived. Bud was able to hunt, fish, and explore the old dumps around the area to dig for bottles. He also liked to explore the hills around the old gold claims. We had two black-cherry trees on our lots that had more fruit than ever was used. We ended up making wine from them, as Bud hated to see the fruit go to waste on the ground. Before we were finished, we had experimented with most of the local fruits, and I had even made up a batch of dandelion wine. Most of the selections were very flavorful, and all were potent.

Dandelion Wine

Butter-yellow discs
That leave gold upon my hand
Are gathered by the gallon,
Steeped slowly in syrup and yeast,
Reduced to a milk-white liquid;
Then bottled for a year.

Trapped within the bottle
White sediment descends,
Leaving in golden amber
Summer's essence to imbibe,
Memories of sun-warmed days
Caught within a crystal glass.

In 1972, Bud decided that he wanted a horse to use for hunting. One of the men who worked with him had two, a filly and a gelding, that he would sell. One Saturday, Bud took Stepper, the gelding, and I was up on Cindy, the red dun filly. She was not the dull grey-brown of most duns. She was bright with a dark red mane and tail as well as the dun's stripe along her spine. We headed into the sagebrush hills north of town. My riding experience was very limited. I had been on my brother-in-law's horse, Bonnie, when Bud had taken care of her at Kimberly, and had been on one other horse. Still, I was confident I could handle Cindy. She was a small horse. We spent most of the day roaming the hills with the two horses keeping pace with each other. I really think I was along for the ride. Cindy was more in control than I was. Looking back, I shudder at the chances we took with no thought to gopher holes and possible stumbles or injuries as we raced through the sagebrush across the hills.

We worked our way back to town by late afternoon, and Bud decided to buy Cindy. Only later, along with the aches and pains of muscles not used to riding, did I discover just what owning a horse really meant. It only took $150 to purchase her, but we had no saddles or tack, and neither of us knew much about caring for a horse. Bud had not even located pasture to rent. Before the year was out, we learned about horseshoes and vet bills, too. Where do you find a good farrier? The one we chose tied Cindy to an apple tree, where she managed to throw herself and cut open one knee. That meant a veterinary visit on the scene. We had sufficient grass around the mobile home to keep her close until we could locate pasture, but the low, split-rail fencing with drive-through space would not hold a horse. Then we learned that a concrete block was not heavy enough for a tether. Neither was a toolbox filled with tools. Talk about a clatter! Every move she made created more noise and scared her into a panic. That meant treatment for a bad rope burn on her chest. She also tore open the stitches on her knee. Now she needed antibiotic shots for the knee and an anti-inflammatory to ease the chest swelling. By the time we finished treating her, she shied from any man who came near her wearing a western hat.

We arranged to pasture Cindy on the empty lots next to us where water was available with adequate grass and good shade. At first, I did not spend much time with her as she was supposed to be Bud's hunting horse. However, he did not get a saddle and tack for her and never spent time with her. I borrowed a saddle so that I could ride her, but as the saddle was too big for me. I lost my stirrups and found myself on the ground when she came to a sudden stop. Because her previous owner had used her for arena racing, all she knew how to do was run. I could see that it would take time and work before I would really feel secure with her.

The Red Dun Mare

Against the evening sky
She stands:
A dark silhouette,
A moment of silence,
With head flung high,
Nostrils flaring,
Ears pricked forward
To catch the faint motor whine.

A passing breeze
Caresses and lifts
The red mane and tail
Breaking the stillness.

Twilight listens
And understands when
The iron-shod feet
Thud against the trail
To the house.

Because I knew nothing about caring for horses, I began looking for books and magazines to help me. Charlie Short, who worked at the experiment station, trained horses, and did horseshoeing. When I had problems with her, I would talk to him. Then I began looking for a saddle. At the saddle shop in La Grande, I finally found an old turn-of-the-century saddle that fit me. It was not just old—it was ancient, but I liked the high pommel and horn in front and the high cantle in back that formed a seat just right for me. It would hold me securely as long as I kept my stirrups. There was no way I could fall out of that old saddle. Also, it was light enough that I could easily toss it on the horse. I would use this saddle until there was no seat left and the saddle maker said it was not worth restoring.

I now had the basic equipment for riding whenever I could make time between work and home. Cindy was a two-year-old, and I quickly realized that meant that she did not know much. Neither did I, but we kept at it and learned together.

Bud took Cindy hunting once on a winter elk hunt. Come to find out, the men were riding in deep snow and rough country. When she lay down with him, he decided she was not big enough for the job. The only thing wrong with Cindy was her youth and stamina. She was just not up to the work he expected of her. Needless to say, his interest in her lessened, but we still had a horse.

Gradually, I spent more and more time with her; with help from Charlie I became a better rider, and Cindy learned what was expected of her. When she became balky and I did not know what to do, Charlie would climb aboard and work out the kinks. She became my horse after that. With everything I had to occupy my time, there was not a lot of time to ride, but I did manage some.

As a three-year-old, Cindy was more than my inexperience could cope with. When I rode her along the lanes where cattle were grazing, she would shy and fight the bit. Charlie switched her from a snaffle bit to a bosal—a braided, rawhide loop with a knot under the chin—that seemed to work better for a while, but she would still balk around cows. Finally, Charlie took her to the Hall Ranch to work cattle.

Before I left the office the first day the cattle were worked at the Hall Ranch, my boss Marty came in saying, "I don't know what you think is wrong with your mare. She did just fine."

"You should have seen her with that old bull," the foreman added. "She just chested right up to him and shoved him along. And she put that old palomino of Marty's to shame."

"Yah," Charlie interrupted. "Our horses were dragging tail when we got to the corral, but that mare still had her head up looking for more cows to push."

Two or three weeks of work made a big difference. She had a job to do and someone experienced to ride her. The next change was to place her in a light mechanical hackamore that gave me more control of her. I kept her in it from then on.

Besides learning to ride and care for a horse, I learned about pasture rent, hay for the winter, grain, veterinary expenses, shoes, and then stud fees if she was bred. It all added up. The first time that we had her bred was to a chocolate palomino named Cowboy Leo, a well-muscled quarter horse that did not look his age. The breeding took, and eventually Cindy birthed Tam, a palomino filly that was the last foal sired by Cowboy.

Following a second breeding, Cindy was due to foal in April of 1975. This time we had taken her to Johnny Ray, a thoroughbred stallion. In April, even though spring had come to the valley floor, our pasture was still snow covered. Because I was afraid she would lose the colt if she foaled in such a situation, I arranged to board her with the vet who lived near Island City. Early in the month, I rode her down the mountain. Then I stopped each evening on my way home from work to feed, water, and exercise her. This continued into May when she dropped her foal, a little stud colt that I named Thunder for the way he raced around. He was dark brown with a black mane, tail, and stockings. Again, I called on Charlie and his trailer to move the mother and baby home.

November Dance

Ice glazes the pools and rocks;
Snow whitens late grasses.
My breath becomes fog
As I heave the saddle to her back.

Her russet coat, no long satin,
Is furred with velvet,
Warm to fingers clad in elk skin.

She snorts as I draw the cinch,
Tosses her head, paws eagerly
Her new-shod hoof thudding
On fresh frozen sod.

She sidles as I gather reins,
Stretches her slender neck,
And dances away
To do what she does best.
"'Tis time," the neighbor said,
"To separate the cows. If you'll
Help, we'll send Spook home again."
(Spook, that wily heifer, preferred not solitude.
She'd breached the fence and disappeared.)

The meadow lies before us
Peopled with dozing cows and calves.
Cindy takes one long look,
Flicks an ear and nods.

I double-check the cinch,
Tighten it another notch;
No need for slipping saddle

When footing becomes uncertain.

Through the gate, she speeds,
Each step lighter than the last.
She circles way around
Beyond the farthest pair.
Then with feet awhirl
She dances, two steps right;
One left.
The cows begin to move.

She dodges, twists,
Retraces each and every step.
I stay astride, a passenger.
She spins; I tilt;
She falters as I right.

Off again, nervous lather wetting her chest,
Ears erect, eyes bright,
Hooves glancing from hummock to spur.
First, the circle round;
Then a minuet.
She partners each and every pair
Through dip and glide
Until the final pavane
And curtsy at the barn.

While all of this was happening, Bud bought a white Jeep four-by-four pickup and an unfinished house on five acres near Morgan Lake, two miles above La Grande. Our friends, Jim and Geri Hall had purchased a home adjoining this property, and Jim convinced Bud that the five acres was a bargain. The original house had burned and been partially rebuilt. There was an old apple orchard, and water was provided by a spring that supposedly had sufficient water as long as the holding tank was kept full. We could use the barn that existed, but it was not part of our purchase.

I was comfortable at Union, and for once in my life felt that we were getting our feet under us. We both had jobs and were able to pay our bills and had begun to save part of our earnings. Still, I liked the idea of a bigger piece of ground. The house was located at the edge of timbered land, and on a clear day, standing on the front deck, I could look across the Grande Ronde Valley, sixty-five miles north, to the Washington hills.

We were busy. Didi spent much time with Mother during this period. At first I fed and rocked her each morning. Later, Mother would come to the trailer to be there when Didi awoke. Most afternoons, and always in the evenings, I had time with her. Jobs filled the days, and during after-work hours, while we salvaged lumber from the house that Bud had purchased at Ladd Marsh, Didi was with Mother. Bud did the major demolition, but as we hoped to reuse the lumber, we had to pull all of the nails from the boards. Dad and I spent evening hours pulling and pounding out the used nails. Then, we loaded the cleaned lumber into the pickup and hauled it to Morgan Lake to use in finishing the house.

The new house had been built using the original foundation. That meant it was a small house for us. There were two adequate bedrooms, a bath, a large living room, and a large country kitchen. Bud decided to add a double garage and shop space as well as a walk-in cellar. For two years, he spent most of his spare time working on this house. Even then, it was not completely finished when we moved in, late in 1973.

Before the actual move, we had to find furnishings, as the mobile home did not have everything we would need. I found a walnut bedroom set at the North Powder auction, and bought a recliner and single bed from Dr. MacArthur when he retired and moved. I bought a used washer and dryer set, kitchen appliances, and a table and chairs. We moved as soon as we acquired all the necessary furnishings. I liked the Morgan Lake property as it was out of town, located high in the hills (at least thirty-five hundred feet in elevation). We now had five acres that gave room for the horses, too, although I found I hated the daily commute to work in Union when the weather was bad.

Bud had purchased another horse, Queen, an American Saddlebred that he thought would be large enough for his needs. I rode her from the Union pasture to the Morgan Lake place on a Saturday, but we had Charlie haul Cindy and Tam, the foal, as Tam was too small to walk the distance. We settled in with two mares, the foal, Beau, a parti-colored poodle that had been returned to us, Sheba the Siamese, and Callie the Manx, who had adopted us in Union. After moving, we acquired Bapé, a registered Japanese poodle, from the Multnomah County Humane Society, and two red Irish setters, Brandy and Murph. By now, Koki was blind and lost anywhere but with Mother and Dad. Mother nursed him through one more winter before I had to take him to the vet. This was very difficult for me, and Didi insisted on seeing him one last time when I brought him home. She kissed him on his fuzzy head before we buried him in the rose garden at Union.

I Die Too

Tears, salty and scalding, blind me
While a huge lump in my throat
Chokes all speech.

I hold you close, watching your fine grey
Fur fall before the clipper's blade.
I see Death's needle probe for your life,
And remember your once eager
Bounce of welcome,
Your brown eyes alight with love.

I cradle you, now deaf and unseeing
But still trusting
Me—who calls death Mercy.
Understand. . .
I love you.

After the move, I drove back and forth to Union, leaving Didi with Mother during the day while I worked. Once winter weather arrived, I left my car parked on the last paved street near Morgan Lake Road, and Didi and I rode up the mountain with Bud in the Jeep CJ5 that he now had. From town to our place was only two miles, but it was an uphill grade, steep and slick with packed ice and snow in bad weather.

At work, I was having trouble with my right wrist. It also was painful to pick up Didi. At first, Dr. Rose treated me with cortisone and immobilization. When that did not relieve the pain, I underwent carpal tunnel surgery. All in all, I wore a brace or a cast for twelve weeks. By the time I was finally able to remove the wraps, I had learned how to write with my left hand. Even the bank accepted a left-handed signature on my checks. That was good. The downside was losing my closeness with Didi because she turned to Daddy and Grandma when she wanted held. She would climb into my lap, but that just wasn't the same.

My job was varied but not intellectually demanding or stimulating, and I could see that using the office machines bothered my wrist. I began looking for career alternatives. I did not qualify for a disability, yet I had no other career training. I returned to school to acquire the teaching credentials that I had ignored previously. To accommodate class hours, I reduced my working time to .80 F.T.E. (full time employment), which allowed me to schedule classes and work in a flexible schedule. I ate a sandwich while working or while driving from the classroom to the office. I took early or late classes and still put in my hours at work. This routine began in September 1974 as I began the required education courses needed for the basic teaching certificate. The next step would be for the standard certificate, the equivalent of another master's degree, but I did not need the thesis. By then I had reached a point where I no longer had to prove to myself or anyone else that I had a mind and was smart enough to succeed. Therefore, even though I had earned the equivalent of a second degree, I only have one.

I went back to school not really knowing if teaching was the best choice. I did know that I enjoyed sharing with others what I had learned. I also knew that it was not likely that I would be able to continue with work that stressed my right wrist. Because I had always liked books and had majored in English, I chose to certify in language arts. Discovering that I could write was the biggest change for me during this time. During undergraduate years, I had become an adequate writer able to earn A's from my professors when I submitted term papers. However, for teaching requirements, I still needed additional coursework. Because no writing course fit into my schedule, I signed up for a directed writing class with George Venn, who was the resident poet/writer on campus. I told him, "Give me anything except creative writing." Yet where did I find myself?

Right smack in the middle of a poetry class. I just knew I could never write poetry; however, to my surprise as I began to write from models, I learned that I could manipulate words on paper. I decided that it would not kill me to learn how to write a poem, especially since I might have to teach students how to do this. By the end of that thirteen-week class, I discovered that I actually could write poetry and have enjoyed doing so ever since.

The next quarter I went on to take Venn's short-story class with the same thought in mind. If I went through the process, I would find it easier to teach creative writing to students. These experiences made me realize that I did have a facility with words, but without stories in my head, I remained a poet, not a teller of tales.

As I continued to develop my skills in Venn's classes, I wrote a children's book for Didi—my version of *The Night before Christmas*. I also began a novel based on my life. At the same time, my job honed my editorial eye. Because the experiment station was a research facility for Oregon State University, those on staff who held doctoral degrees were required to publish on a regular basis. Part of my job as secretary was to edit and prepare the manuscripts for submission to professional journals. In addition, I accepted responsibility for the newsletter put out by the Union County Museum Society. I focused on county history, local architecture, and items of interest to members.

Chapter 9: Whispers of Discontent

When I finished my basic teacher training in 1976, I was still working at the experiment station in Union. At that time, my master's degree and no teaching experience placed me so high on the salary scale that local school districts could not afford to hire me. I applied elsewhere, including Missouri. Bud's cousin John sent a job list for that area from his college. I applied to two or three districts, and Dixon Reorganized School District phoned me but wanted a personal interview. I flew to Missouri for an interview, accepted the position, and rented a house.

When I stepped off the plane in Pendleton and told Bud that I had the job, he said, "You took the job?" He had encouraged me to apply, but never believed I would accept. We listed the Morgan Lake house, and it sold to the first prospective buyer. Because Bud did not ride Queen, we had sold her earlier in the spring. Now, I advertised the others because I could not train Tam or Thunder and did not want to move Cindy and board her in open pasture with a stud when I would have little time to spend with her.

For the actual move, John came to Oregon to help us. He drove the U-Haul truck, towing a trailer, with Brandy, the red setter, beside him on the seat—she later became his dog. Bud, with Beau, had the pickup and camper, and I drove the Mazda station wagon with Didi, Bapé, and Sheba. The Manx cat had gone wild that spring, and Murph, the other red setter, found a new home. On August 19, 1976, we were in Dixon, Missouri, and I was in charge of my first classroom.

It was a very different world, but I was never bored. Didi, at five and one half, entered kindergarten that fall, and my neighbor, Rhonda kept her until I finished my day at school. When I began teaching at Dixon High School, I did not know that I could be a teacher. Other than my student teaching in La Grande and my fifteen-year-old niece, Sandra, who spent one year with us, I had very little experience with teenagers. Suddenly, I found myself immersed in one of the most challenging experiences of my life.

I asked Mr. Spurlock, the principal, about the curriculum I was to use. He said, "That's why you were hired. The textbooks are all stacked in the library." I surveyed my materials and began. I had grades ten, eleven, and twelve for English, a speech class, and a publications class for newspaper and yearbook. I was literally starting from scratch with no guidelines from the previous year. That first year I taught grammar, literature, and writing in the English classes. I added a unit on writing the short story for the twelfth grade. Once my classes were underway, I began to create a program of units for the upcoming year, looked at materials and selected new books, put on the school play, and began planning a literary publication. Meanwhile, Bud headed back to Oregon. He returned for Christmas, bringing an eight-foot Christmas tree for the new house.

I had rented a comfortable two-bedroom house that was adequate and affordable; however, by the time the sale of the Oregon house closed and Bud was able to invest those monies in antique sales, he saw the bank account depleting faster than he liked. He decided that we needed to invest in a house instead of rent. I preferred owning a home rather than renting, but I did not want to purchase one when he gave all indications of not living in Missouri. Still, we looked at those available, chose one of the older but nicer ones, and moved in just before Christmas. The price was reasonable, and the house was located on a corner lot with large oaks and a pecan tree. I liked the house, even though the furnace went out the first winter and the roof leaked over the main bedroom. I could not do the repairs, and Bud was not there to do any of it. He had returned to Oregon, leaving me with Didi.

Although Bud says he returned to a job from which he had taken leave, I remember that the job was completed. He worked sporadically on jobs obtained through the carpenters' local, spent time starting the building we had planned for the Union property, and tried to sell the antiques that he had purchased in Missouri for resale in Oregon.

When school finished in May 1977, I packed Didi and the animals into my Mazda station wagon and headed back to Oregon for a session of summer school. I still needed to complete work for a standard teaching certificate and now had to focus classes on speech for Missouri certification, as that was one of my assigned teaching areas. Because the school play was another of my assignments, I also picked up theater production classes.

We stayed with Mom and Dad in Union when I first returned, but it was not long before Bud and I went shopping and bought a nineteen-foot travel trailer. He must have lived with them that winter, but I just don't remember. The trailer was tight quarters but sufficient for the summer as we were not all in it together most of the time. Didi stayed next door with her grandmother quite often. Bud used it for living quarters when Didi and I returned to Missouri.

She and I returned for school in early August of 1977 to find that the luxuriant strawberry patch had burned up for lack of water. Our neighbor Rhonda had been irrigating for me, but a sudden hot spell defeated her. That August was very hot and humid. If the house had not had central air conditioning, I would have been miserable until cooler weather moved in.

I was eager to return to school, and Didi wanted to rejoin her playmates and Rhonda. I did not miss Oregon because I was involved in a new, engrossing career and surrounded by friendly neighbors. I enjoyed my students and developed friendships with Marge the counselor, Bill the science teacher, and several others. Besides that, trips with the speech team and my extracurricular activities filled my hours if I was not reading student papers at home. Didi went with me on these trips, my students treating her like a little sister, even coloring with her.

I taught three English classes, speech/drama, publications, and tutored a student who was pregnant. Before the year was over, I had produced Dixon's first literary magazine, *Wildfire*, prodded students through the spring play, and planned and hosted a district-wide speech tournament.

Bud flew to Missouri for Christmas and stayed two weeks before returning to Oregon where he remained until I resigned in May. He flew back to help us move. I never really understood why he did not like Missouri. He seemed to anticipate the move until I took the job. Then something changed. Once there, he did not like the climate, and he did not like the open-shop working situation where he had to go to jobsites rather than to a union hall. He thoroughly enjoyed the auctions and attended three or four every week when he was there. I would go along to some of them, leaving Didi with Rhonda and taking an attaché case full of papers to grade. Still, he could not settle to make a home there, so I left. That was hard for me, as I took deep pleasure in my home, my job, the kids, and the people of Dixon. I regretted leaving. However, I knew I would not have a marriage if I stayed in Dixon.

I never really thought of my life as full of travail or problems, and I never recognized that being happy was not a major part of my life. I was too busy filling my time with child, school, work, my home activities, and/or genealogy to realize I was missing a great deal. I think I simply took things as they came and tackled them head on. There was always a sense of something missing, but it took years for me to discover what it was.

The summer of 1978 was difficult for me. Bud was out of work, and I had just left a job I enjoyed. I had packed a home into boxes and placed it in storage. Didi and I spent the summer with Bud in the travel trailer at Union while I finished work for my standard certificate. Nevertheless, something was not right. I felt like an outsider—unwanted and intruding. I would often find my teenage niece in the trailer when I returned from school, and I felt as if I was walking into a room just as everyone quit talking—and the silence was thick enough to cut with a knife.

Extra work for a technical writing class and a theater class made this summer more intensive than previous sessions. I finished the school day tired with several hours of reading or writing to complete, but I could not concentrate in the tense atmosphere. Finally, I told

Sandra not to come around unless I was present. Then I tried to explain to Bud how I felt. He verbally jumped all over me, saying, "I don't agree with your ideas. Not everyone needs an education. Besides, I don't see any value in what you are doing." He repudiated everything I was working toward. I felt rejected as well.

The emotional stress on top of the school pressure and my need to find another job sent me back to my doctor. I asked for a prescription of Meprobamate to get me through the rest of the summer. Because it gave me an edge of control that kept me from crying all the time, he let me have it. It helped me handle the job interviews that I hoped would provide a position for the upcoming school year.

School went well, and I finished my required studies for my standard certificate, including the technical writing class that had given me a new perspective that was neither poetry nor fiction. Jobs were scarce around the La Grande area, and I was applying across the state. I had interviews throughout the summer but still nothing in the Union/La Grande area. Among others, I interviewed at Scio, located south of Salem, and at Roseburg and Klamath Falls in the southern part of the state. Bud gave me no help, one way or another, in choosing a location. It was as if he was a bystander—leaving the entire choice to me. Eventually, I accepted a position at Bonanza High School, twenty-five miles east of Klamath Falls.

Bud's sister, Carol Lee, had been house hunting for us and had located a rental not far from where she lived in the south suburb area of Klamath Falls. The house was close to Ferguson Elementary, and both were within a short walking distance of Carol's home. Deidre could leave her school, cross the street, and cut through the pasture behind the church to her aunt's home after school. We rented the house and lived at the Bel Aire Drive address for just over a year. I commuted twenty-five miles to Bonanza where I taught English and speech to grades seven, ten, eleven, and twelve.

Bud found work hit and miss in the local area and then went to work for a friend who had a hospital remodeling project in Coeur d'Alene, Idaho. He was there in 1979 when our landlord decided that she wanted her house back. I really did not want to purchase a home, as I was not particularly enamored with this part of Oregon. Owning a home would make it harder if I wanted to move to another school district. Even so, Carol Lee and I, again, began house hunting, eventually finding a lovely home that we both liked; however, it was more money than Bud's GI loan would finance. That took some creative financing, but eventually I was able to put the purchase together, even though I always felt overextended with the expenses.

That house on Independence Avenue was the largest I had ever lived in—about sixteen hundred square feet, but it took the large antique furniture that we had acquired in Missouri and had room for my baby grand piano that was still with Mother in Union. The L-shaped house had three bedrooms and two baths in one leg of the L, and a foyer, formal living room, large, open kitchen-dining-family-room area, and an oversized garage in the other leg of the L. The piano occupied one corner of the living room, keeping company with two curved-front china cabinets, an oak organ, and the Victorian settee and chair that I recovered in garnet-colored velvet. This house became a showcase for the antiques that Bud bought in Missouri and in the years that followed.

In March of 1980, my father's health took a downturn. He had been coping with Parkinson's disease and what was called "hardening of the arteries" at the time. He walked with difficulty and shuffled instead of striding out. His memory continued to fail more each year, which was very hard for him to accept. Just before spring break came that March, Mother called to tell me Dad was dying. She had called Ruth in Portland and Georgia in Arkansas. By the time I arrived in Union, both of them were there.

Dad raved and ranted in hallucination. Mother's minister provided moral support and prayed for Dad's release. Dad tossed with apparent fever, his attention focused on the wall beyond the foot of the cot where he lay. Mother had set it up in the living room for him because it was awkward getting him into their bedroom.

He spoke of flames, a bright light, and someone calling him. Variations of this continued throughout the first night as he clung tightly to life. I sat with him and cried because I could do nothing for him. Letting him go hurt—he was the one stable rock in the river of my life. Still, I wanted him to let go and find peace.

For a break, Ruth and I sat on the front steps while she smoked a cigarette. The stars shone brightly in a midnight sky, and we both shivered as an unseen presence passed between us—moving out of the house. Power withdrew, leaving quietness behind.

"Did you feel that?" Ruth asked.

"Yes. I wonder what it was."

Inside, Dad's breathing eased, but he did not rally. The next evening Ruth, Georgia, and I drove into La Grande to Grizzly Bear Pizza, taking time over food to discover the changes in our lives. Ruth and I ordered wine, but a single glass did not touch the hurting inside. By the time we left, both of us were tipsy. Georgia was horrified. The wine helped for a short time, but the intensity of emotions continued. Mother was sure that Dad was dying, but he did not—not for five long years more.

He remained bedfast from that point until his death in 1985, which in a way came as a relief. I had said my good-byes in 1980. Now he was free, and so were we. During the last years of his illness, Mother learned to pick up the reins and manage their lives. Up to that time, she had always relied more on Daddy than on herself.

After I returned to the classroom, I applied for a transfer to Brixner Junior High in Klamath Falls. I had sent in the application but had not talked to my principal. Before I could tell him, he told me he had given me a good report. Brixner Junior High had over five hundred seventh- and eighth-graders enrolled during my first year there. I was a five-minute drive from the house, and Deidre walked three blocks to her elementary school.

During the summer, my Mazda RX-3 station wagon began to have serious problems. Meanwhile, I had pulled the tendons in my right arm using a line trimmer in the yard. I was wearing a cast and would not be driving for two weeks. Therefore, I took the vehicle to the dealership for diagnosis and repair. They could have the car until I needed it for school. One thing led to another—the shop replaced the ignition and I do not remember what else. Then they told me it was the carburetor—but they could not guarantee that a new one would fix the problem. I had already decided the next car would be a Mazda 626, a two-door coupe, but I was just not ready to give up that little station wagon. Now, school was starting and I needed wheels.

The dealership had two versions of the car I wanted: renaissance red with black trim, or gold with tan trim.

Both had air conditioning and a stick shift, but I was unable to get a salesman to be serious with me until Bud made a phone call from Portland where he was working. I guess he promised the guy a steak dinner. At any rate, I got the deal I wanted and went home with the red car. I hate it when a man thinks that I am not capable of thinking logically or buying a car for myself.

Teaching junior high was a real change for me, but also it was easier, as I did not have to jump mentally from that level to high-school-age kids. However, the transfer to another school brought its own problems. In November of 1980, I encountered school politics in a way that shook me to the foundation of my values. At the end of the first quarter grading period, I figured the grades for my classes and was ready to enter the scores on computer sheets for the district office. I had tallied all of my classes and figured the percentage of students achieving each letter grade. The results did not fit the normal curve that has roughly 7 percent failure and most of the scores in the 70 percent or above range. My figures showed a 43 percent failure rate. Because I had never had this happen before, I questioned my abilities as a teacher. In passing, I mentioned this to another teacher over lunch.

Later in the day, the principal came to my room and asked about the percentage of F's in my classes. I told him what I had found, and he told me that was too many.

He also told me to rank all the scores in a curve. This would lower the performance expectation and allow more students to pass. He said, "You are too good a teacher to face the trouble with parents for flunking that many students." He added, "Parents don't expect failure!" I explained that I had previously contacted parents with few results. Then he said, "It is district policy to grade on curves, and if you don't grade this way, you will be too different. Brixner already has enough problems." To add insult to injury, he added, "I'm not telling you how to grade; you can still use points or percentages, but you must fit the expected curve." I felt as if he had physically hit me in the pit of my stomach. The tears came, as usual, when I'm under stress. I did as he asked—ranked my percents and broke them into a curve. He approved, and I altered my grades.

After school was over for the day, I took Wilma, my mother-in-law, shopping. Because I was tense, my shoulders were tight. I felt that I had no one with whom I could share the distress. I wanted a couple of strong drinks, to swear, or to hit out. I did none of those. Finally, at bedtime, I cried. Then I took a Meprobamate tablet and slept.

The next morning I awoke with an excruciating sinus headache. I took my medication for the pressure and an Empirin with codeine for the pain. That upset my stomach, and I went back to bed. At ten thirty, I managed some toast and at two thirty, a sandwich. The rest of the time, I slept—still sick. At six thirty that evening, I finally felt like moving and was up until eleven when I again went to bed, but for a restless night. Sunday morning I still had a headache but no longer felt sick. Following a hot shower and breakfast, Deidre and I went shopping for groceries and new boots for her. I pushed away my discomfort as I ironed clothes and completed other weekend chores. Finally, though, I gave in and called my friend Jean Davies who was the school counselor at Bonanza. She came over and listened as I talked.

What I had done at the school runs counter to all I believe. My personal values demand high expectations and personal accountability. I cannot pass students who are incompetent just to play it safe. I told Jean that, realizing this, I also knew that I was physically sick because of my actions. It was a way to cope or escape. To resolve the conflict, I must compromise my beliefs (I couldn't), continue to grade my way, or not give grades at all. We talked about what was at stake. I felt strongly enough to quit my job, but then I would jeopardize my personal goals and all I had struggled to attain. That meant I needed an alternative. We spoke of an OEA grievance procedure or of taking the issue to the district assistant superintendent. Even so, that would jeopardize my future as a teacher in the district, as this was the year I would attain permanent status. My only remaining choice would be not to give grades.

We discussed this as a method that worked with older students, although the teacher who attempts it leaves herself wide open and risks much. Jean emphasized that guiding the students to set their goals and ways of measurement would involve group process, a learning experience in itself. In addition, I thought that students taking responsibility for their grades would be a step toward maturity, and if we were successful, I would win in the end. After all, students giving themselves grades they don't deserve would be no different than using a curve to lower the failing point. It would, however, let me off the hook. On the positive side, I felt at peace when we finished talking, my energy had returned, and the headache was gone.

**

Journal entry, June 4, 1981

Everyone Needs a Dream

To some, dreams are goals to be attained, fights to be won, challenges to be met, or perhaps a star to be plucked. Not all dreams are of this stuff. Some dreams are a searching where you seek without finding, yearn without satisfying, and ask yourself what exactly it is that you keep reaching for.

You marry, but that is not the answer. Although you belong to another, you still feel alone. For a time, you seek achievement in study and experience the thrill that comes through learning and grappling with others' minds and ideas. Then that too pales. In work, you seek perfection, to be the most efficient, the best, but you become bored with the routine and repetition.

Eventually, a child is born, and you learn the heights of joy and the depths of pain. You hold him close, give him the breast and know peace. Too soon, you plummet to the depths of sorrow and loss because he dies. Again, you are alone.

Sorrow passes as does all winter, and as it goes, a new life is born. You nurture her, and she thrives. You experience the wonder of this tiny being that can captivate, frustrate, and exhaust you. As she grows, you are too busy to be alone, too tired to wonder about the future.

Yet the future becomes today. The child is an individual with her own wants, needs, and ideas. You become aware of yourself and your needs. You are still alone. There is satisfaction from things you do, in jobs well done, and in projects finished, yet you want more.

You have learned to live, mostly alone, and you have come to like the independence, the lack of conflict, and the doing for yourself. Yet there are times you reach out, and no one is there to hold you. You realize suddenly one night that the qualities you seek—quiet strength that's always behind you, caring and concern, willingness to listen without judging, the will to challenge you to grow and become more because you can—are missing in the man you married. You want a man who will stand beside you but who is strong enough to relate to as an equal. It is then you have reached a turning, but to what? Dreams are many things. Some are realized; others are as gossamer, almost impossible to grasp.

**

During the next year at Brixner, I became interested in the Oregon Writing Project and in the summer of 1981, took a summer session at Southern Oregon College. Deidre was quite willing to spend this time between home and her aunt Carol's. This project taught teachers to be writers with students and to use the writing process across the curriculum, not just in English classes. I had continued to write poetry but had not returned to fiction. This session gave me a chance to write without home interruptions and to see how other teachers were using writing in their classrooms. We wrote and shared as a group. I learned that I could write when someone else took care of the household details. Bud was working in Portland, and Deidre was with Carol Lee. I ate in a cafeteria and had no responsibilities other than my classes. Truly, an unrealistic situation for a woman with a home, child, and job, but it worked for me. I wrote "Sanctuary," that was published in *Oregon English*, and the short story, "Sometimes a Cold Wind." This class changed the way I taught. I no longer taught grammar, composition, and literature. Now, I focused on writing as a process. I wove the grammar and spelling into the writing, and students learned composition skills as they wrote about literature.

Sanctuary

I have a picture…
Green-white, the water tumbling
On a rushing mountain stream
Over green-black rocks
Around fallen trees.

Tall firs, like sentinels, stand
On guard.
Frail ferns and scarlet leaves vie
Under bare birch limbs

Torrent and tumult, yet…
Peace.

When I felt comfortable with my work at Brixner, I returned to genealogy. Leola Thompson, friends I had made through the LDS Family History Center, and I attended a workshop that sparked interest in forming our own group, so I led in the formation of the Klamath Basin Genealogical Society. Leola Thompson, a member of the local chapter of Daughters of the Revolution and Daughters of the Colonists, encouraged me to research and document Mother's line for membership in both societies. Pursuit of this information taught me the basics of family research. Searching for records on my great-great-grandfather Schuyler Rue led me to Linkville Cemetery, the earliest cemetery in Klamath Falls. With the caretaker's help, I located records and found the grave, identified only by a small round metal marker.

This experience led to a cemetery project for the genealogical society. The cemetery district recorded names on plot maps, but when I asked about a file or printed records, the caretaker said, "DAR started to read the cemetery once, but it is just too big. No one will ever read it all." As that was a challenge I could not resist, I took this need to the society. As a group, we committed ourselves to reading every stone in Linkville Cemetery. Deidre accompanied me on many of my visits to the cemetery, adding her carefully written notes to mine. I took the handwritten notes made by members as they copied inscriptions and made card entries, creating a file to compare with the plot records. In this process of cross-checking, I found many questionable entries. Our work then led to errors corrected and missing entries completed. Later, I typed the manuscript, and the society published volume I of the *Klamath Basin Cemetery Records*. Volume II followed after we read outlying burial sites and acquired records from the local Indian authorities.

In 1981, Bud bought a Honda Prelude to reduce transportation expenses as the Chevrolet pickup that he drove definitely drank its share of gasoline. Then, he went from work in Coeur d'Alene, Idaho, to a job in the Seattle area. After that, he spent eighteen months mostly unemployed, holding brief jobs in the Klamath area but nothing permanent. This was a hard period for all of us. Deidre and I were not used to having him at home, and as he tried to be comfortable and make it his home, we experienced many tensions. I spent much time with research, and she holed up in her bedroom with a radio.

When school was out in June of 1982, Bud and I took a week's trip to Kansas. Deidre had never particularly enjoyed traveling and chose to visit with friends in Sandpoint, Idaho, instead. I enjoyed the drive through the mountains of northern Idaho and through Yellowstone. From there we went to Deer Lodge, Montana, and stopped to visit with my youngest sister Georgia, who had lived there since her husband's discharge from the air force. They began their life together in Ohio, spent time in Arkansas, Alaska, and Colorado Springs, winding up in Montana.

With only a week for travel, we did not stay long in any one place. Our main destination was an antique shop in Phillipsburg, Kansas, a place we had spotted one other time we were through that area. It was an older building, chock-full of dusty merchandise. It did not appear to be a thriving business. Somehow, by asking the right questions, we finally located a woman who could let us look at things. We left there with a *Gone with the Wind* lamp that had a satin glass base and shade, a purple, carnival-glass dresser tray in the grape pattern, and other things that I cannot recall. One other stop was to look at another piece of carnival glass—a stag-and-holly bowl in marigold. Carnival glass is an iridescent glass originally made in the 1920s and sold cheaply or given as prizes—hence the name. I bought the bowl there, as well as a composition baby doll. Bud had a passion for antiques and collectibles. I enjoyed the adrenaline rush of taking a bid, and I loved some of the antiques. However, I was picky with my purchases. I limited myself to items that I could live with, while Bud thought about flea-market resale. I enjoyed collecting the rarer pieces of glass, but quantity meant more to Bud.

That same summer, on July 15, 1982, Bud and I backpacked into his gold claim on the John Day River for the second time. This was too difficult a trek for

Deidre, now age eleven, so she was again with her aunt. I did not care about panning for gold or fishing, but I wanted to spend time in the mountains and along the river. This time we took the trail south along the river, which was a much easier hike than the Silver Butte Trail we had hiked the year before. After leaving the pickup at North Fork Campground, we hiked for seven-and-a-half hours to cover the eight miles between the campground and Bud's gold claim on the river.

The John Day River was at least two feet higher than the previous summer—clear, green-white, and rapid—a constant roar of rushing water with the occasional *thud, thud*, as water dropped deep over a boulder. The sky was clear, but the temperature remained cool. An errant breeze frequently wandered across the trail, making it a nice time for hiking. Wild flowers, lupine, larkspur, Indian paintbrush, and columbine created bright spots of color where they bloomed. The trail meandered through low-growing huckleberry bushes for most of the distance. These berries, though red in color, were not yet ready to pick, but they had attracted a young brown bear to the slope. His coat was still shaggy and had an unusual, grizzled light-brown color. He was grubbing at a tree just off the trail when we approached. He bolted part of the way up the hill, turned, and reared onto his hind legs to watch us. Then, down he went onto all fours and scrambled up the hill.

That same summer we also found time to visit

the southern Oregon coast, where I bought a Gulick seascape. The artist had a gallery in Port Orford where he painted and displayed his work. I spent at least an hour looking at his paintings. One that captured my attention was a night scene, but I chose another of the waves and spume on the rocks.

Coastal Sunset

Blood red, overlaid with gold,
The perfect orb
Suspended against a patchwork
Of mauve, purple, and gold…

Hesitates

Then plunges into molten waves,
Leaving ripples of crimson,
Tassels of amber.

Night draws a shadowy drape
Dimming the brilliance

But wait

One last ray
Captured
By one lone cloud
Refracts the light,

An aftertaste of pleasure
To be savored.

**

I began journal writing as a tool for counseling sessions as I tried to work through my feelings about Bud and our relationship. In the parking lot of the elementary school after voting in May, Bud's uncle Al said, "I don't know why you stick with him. You know he had another girl when you were pregnant the last time." When asked, Bud had a ready answer to explain away the accusation. Later, when I went to use a notebook that he had given me, I found a card and intimate note—stamped and ready to mail—to an unknown woman in the Portland area. He explained her away as a good friend—nothing serious.

Still, I hurt. Old turmoil rose to the surface, and I no longer believed him. This time I found myself unable to hide from my emotions. I needed to talk—but to whom? Opening the phone book, I selected a number and dialed. Thus began a series of weekly sessions that gave me tools for coping. The habit of journal writing has stayed with me since as a means to work through problems, write poetry, keep travel notes, and record conference information. I recorded in words what I could not share verbally.

Journal Entry, March 29, 1983

Bud is going to Union today, unless I get home to find that something altered his plans. He wanted us to go last week while I was not in school, but I did not want to go. I wouldn't have minded the traveling; I just didn't want to cope with the situation that I would find at Mother's. My depressed mental state leaves no room for the problem of Dad and Mother. She called one evening just to talk and sounded in good spirits, but I could hear Dad yelling in the background. He was having a bad spell.

I guess I feel guilty for not wanting to be with her. I'm selfish. I don't want to have to cope with her problems or the house. I don't have the emotional reserves or strength now. School and having Bud home for so long has left me drained. Deidre feels the tension and spends much of her time in her room with her music, or she goes out with friends. She needs to get away.

I don't feel that we can afford the expense of his trip either. His unemployment has run out. At the same time, I'm thankful for a few days without him. For some reason, I feel restricted, constrained, like I'm walking a tightrope when he is home. A tension builds up. Frustration with his way of doing things, his coffee cups left sitting around, papers left where he was using them, the tracking in from the garage and the patio. His total absorption with television is not new, neither are his other habits. Still, they are a constant rub. It does no good to say anything. He only gets angry and says things that hurt me. I avoid one and try to live with the rest. Right now, his indifference really gets to me. No doubt, he is depressed, too. Extended periods of unemployment are not easy. At the same time, there is little sharing or mutual support. He rarely touches me with a kiss or caress, and when he does, I'm usually uptight and unable to respond. He senses this, I'm sure. The longer he's home, the less loving there seems to be, and I feel worse about our relationship. Worse yet, I cannot talk to him. He thinks that we communicate, but he rarely listens to me. Talk is on safe subjects, superficial comments that skirt real issues and are slipped in during television commercials.

**

Sometime during the summer of 1983, Bud returned to work in Sandpoint, Idaho, on a hospital remodeling job for Hagadone Construction. As a result, we generally saw him at home every other weekend. Many of those times, he came laden with boxes of things he had bought at flea markets or auctions. Occasionally, I'd find interesting odds and ends of sewing notions or fabrics. Sometimes he had carnival glass, and other times he'd come in with collectibles.

During the Christmas holidays of 1983, Deidre, almost thirteen, contracted a virus that was going through the area. Unfortunately, she and a few other children developed complications. The family doctor could find nothing causing her problem, but she didn't get better. By the second visit, he told me it was all in her head and sent us to a child psychiatrist, who listened, checked, rechecked, and ordered an EEG. That's when problems showed up. Deidre needed to go to the Doernbecker Children's Hospital in Portland where they did little other than more tests. The tentative diagnosis was multiple sclerosis. She failed physically to the stage of heart palpitations, and at that point they took her to the cardiac unit and put her on an IV. That was the turning point.

I had said that many of her complaints and symptoms during the illness shouted of low blood sugar. Sure enough, she began to come around when she received some nutrition. In addition, it takes about two weeks for the damaged areas on the nerves to begin to heal. She had one more spell in March 1984, and then nothing more. Doctors said that maybe it was just a central nervous system syndrome.

Bud joined us in Portland (from Idaho) while she was in the hospital, but he gave no emotional support to either of us. He just could not handle the hospital where we had lost Gerry, and he then could not understand my falling apart, as I've always been the strong one.

Everyone pulled at me—I needed to be strong—for Deidre, for Mom and Dad, and for Bud. I stayed with my sister Ruth while Deidre was hospitalized. When the doctors told me they could do nothing for her, she still needed care, and we could go home to Klamath Falls, but all I could do was cry. Ruth lent a shoulder for me to cry on and made an appointment for me with her doctor.

Part III
The Flowering

Chapter 10: Learning to Live

Mind Coils

Rain
cold, grey
tinkling into dark
canyons of the mind:
thoughts.

Thoughts
subtle, hazy
skipping along brain
waves to distant memory:
shadows.

Shadows
indistinct, murky
cloaking, hiding darkness
in which to hide:
Memory.

Deidre became my student when she entered eighth grade. That particular year, I was allowed to create an Honors English class for our academically gifted students, and she qualified with high grades. My class held the top twenty students. I led them through Shakespeare and *The Sword in the Stone*. They learned to write creatively, and we made a class book of their writing. During this time, Deidre wrote, just for me, brief lines hidden inside a wooden apple.

Mom—
Here's an apple for my
favorite teacher

That will never spoil or
rot,
When you look at this
apple
Remember this student
that you taught.

You taught me in school
and you taught me at
home. I hope I never
forget the lessons. They
helped shape my life.
I love you,

Deidre Louise

**

Following her illness, Deidre escaped her world of pain and uncertainty by creating a fantasy character, Kat, in the game Dungeons and Dragons. Then, with her friend Joanne, she joined the Society for Creative Anachronism (SCA), an international organization. She attended wars and tourneys to watch her favorite knights in shining armor fight with rattan swords.

Eventually, she met Dennis of Maplewood at a local event. Dennis Denham became her one-and-only when he was there to pick up the pieces of a fifteen-year-old who was burning the candle at both ends. This was a period of black-leather jackets, motorcycle rides, and boyfriends. She dropped one boyfriend for another who wanted her to become emancipated and move in with him in Portland. She could not support herself, and her father and I would not agree. Her heart was broken when her current flame did not give her the promised engagement ring. Then he did not show up to tell her goodbye. This left her aimless and angry.

Dennis simply waited and watched, and when she crashed—coming down with strep throat at an event—he tucked her into his car and brought her home. After that, he drove from Mt. Shasta, California, to Klamath Falls on weekends to see her and Shadow, Deidre's cat who laid claim to him.

**

In early July 1986, I took a week just for myself to attend a writing workshop. It was titled "Inquiry into Writing," led by Kim Stafford, an instructor at Lewis and Clark College in Lake Oswego. This experience became a retreat of healing as I walked roads shaded by overhanging trees, shared ideas with other writers, and made new friends. In response to a reading selection called "Frameworks," I wrote about Deidre's illness and how I'd responded. Finally, I was able to reach some sort of acceptance, and from that point, I could move forward.

Out to Lunch

I was out to lunch for two years, although I had not stepped out of the framework of a twenty-seven-year marriage. My damage was internal, unseen, and therefore incomprehensible to Bud. My nerves resembled a thread of yarn, shredded and fuzzed by a kitten at play. The electrical impulses did not always cross a synapse correctly, and that left me incapable of analyzing data, learning to use a computer, or creating new projects. I cried under stress and could not cope with loud noises or conflict. Fatigue, when it came, drained me instantly. My brain spun in endless painful loops. I could not decide whether to do or not to do anything. I could not concentrate. My mind had literally shut down.

I spent lots of time doing needlework and genealogy research, although I gathered data that I was incapable of analyzing. I gave up the opportunity to run for the presidency of our local education association and backed off from political and school-related responsibilities. Finally, I stepped down as president of the genealogy group. I continued to work with the society but was no longer responsible for planning programs. Fewer leadership roles made it easier for me to stay on an even keel emotionally. Life went on.

I was a candidate for Dammasch, a mental hospital,

but I did not have the luxury of choosing that escape. Instead, I resumed my day-to-day position as teacher in an eighth-grade English classroom. Because I was a working mother, the daily routine of shutting off the alarm, preparing for work, and meeting each class kept me functioning in the present and moving forward in an attempt to cope with the diagnosis of probable multiple sclerosis handed down for my daughter.

I lay awake in the dark every night, listening for her cough, the faintest hint of breathing as an assurance that she was, in fact, fine. You see, the virus had damaged a microscopic area located in a pea-sized portion of her brainstem. This particular damage affected her swallowing reflex, the left side of her face, and the right side of her body.

If you cannot swallow, you cannot eat—especially soft foods or liquids. She lost twenty pounds, became weak, and experienced heart palpitations. Then her left eyelid drooped and did not function properly. Her mouth froze on that side. Her right arm and leg became weak.

I coped with all of this, including the tests and watching her pain. I became frustrated with doctors who could not find a cause. I ran on adrenaline and sheer nerves until there was nothing left of me. Then I cried and could not stop.

One of the worst things about this time of frayed

nerves was the lack of feelings. I do not know if it was the nerves or the medication, but it was impossible for me to feel anything, and that was very hard on relationships. I did not get angry any more; I did not feel loving or loved. I was just empty. Loneliness never seemed to be a problem—I had Deidre, and aside from her, my own company never bored me. I suppose that my world has always been more of books than of people. Eventually, though, I had to let the inner protective walls crack and take a risk before I was able to react again.

My sister's doctor told me to forget my daughter, to think of myself. But how could I forget her? She held my heart; she was an integral part of me. My world did not revolve around her; instead, she was a major light in my life. In spite of the apparent lack of mothering, she knew I loved her and wanted her for herself, not as a replacement for her brother. I wanted her to be self-reliant, to trust herself, to make her own decisions. In this, she was fortunate to have the care of both her grandmothers and an aunt. They stepped in when I needed to be elsewhere.

That was step one. Each task I did, each day I met, was another step forward. I did not seek for framework, only for escape—escape from my knowledge, my marriage, my job, everything. But there was no escape. I was the wage earner, the insurance provider, and the mother. I rediscovered my journal and wrote. I reentered the world of books and found my way back, one step at a time, one day at a time, until two years later I knew that I needed what a writing workshop could provide: new ideas, new friendships, positive affirmation, and, I hoped, a new start for me into writing.

**

Journal Entry, 1986

The pattern of my life is definitely that of a gyre. I move in circles, but instead of returning to a point of beginning and going in circles as I had thought, I am at the same point on the circle, but higher. If I visualize moving upward on a coiled spring, I can make sense of this pattern and understand how the inner self develops and grows.

Lessons Learned

Merlyn said, "Education is experience, and the essence of experience is self-reliance." On one hand, we learn from everything we participate in, including formal schooling; on the other, we learn by doing. It all depends on how broadly one defines "experience." Self-reliance, however, is the true basis for learning. It is only when one relies on oneself that learning is integrated with past experience and personal habits in such a way as to become memory, something learned.

At the age of forty-four, I think of all the time I have spent in schools and, yes, I have learned a great deal of subject matter and information. I have learned how to study and how to teach. I have learned how to write concisely and fluently, to research, and to ask the right questions in order to obtain the information I desired. I have learned to compete, I have learned persistence and determination, and I have learned to accept my own limitations.

However, the lessons I've learned outside of the classroom have created longer-lasting memories for me. Childhood freedom to roam wild on Top Mountain developed a need within me for open space and an appreciation for the land in its natural state. I have never been an urban dweller at heart. I need a yard, flowers, and a tree. An apartment confines, hems in, and becomes a cage.

As a child, I learned about flatirons and wood ranges—how to keep an even heat for baking or steady pressure on a pressure canner using a wood range. I also learned that my eye-hand coordination made me inept with an axe. Mother attempted to teach me how to chop wood, but my aim was closer to my foot than to the wood. I have never learned to use an axe for splitting, although I can lop branches with one.

I learned to use a needle and thread by sewing for my dolls. I first sewed with paper and then with fabric. Mother taught me to embroider before she let me use the sewing machine. My first experience with a sewing machine was to sew rug strips end to end by using a handle to turn the wheel on the machine before we had electricity. In my teens I made-over, designed, and sewed my own clothes. I did not know that certain fabrics were hard to work with and were better left for experts. I simply sewed. Whether I wanted satin, silk, velvet, or wool plaid, I read directions, worked carefully, and created the garment.

I learned about marriage by being married, discovering that living with someone is different from going with the same person. It was hard to accept a different person than the one I thought I knew. Then I learned about my needs and myself. I need to be wanted, to be busy, to work and create, to succeed.

I learned to be a secretary by getting a job. I knew how to type, to file, and to do basic accounting. That was a start. The rest I learned by doing. Skills are necessary for any job, but the willingness to try something new and the ability to ask for help are far more important. If I know where to find the answer, needed information, or someone who can help me solve a problem, that's more important than remembering or learning all the trivia and details to which I am exposed.

Not all that I have learned came easy. College led me to question the traditional religious beliefs that my parents had taught me. Evolution, archeology, ancient literature—all of these put my Bible learning in a different perspective. I did not quit believing, but I tempered dogma with knowledge. I began to see the fanaticism, the hypocrisy, and the individual prejudices that had molded my faith. I was able to shed the narrow view and accept a more catholic view of religion.

I don't disbelieve now, but I place little value on traditional church routines. I have experienced a power or force that is greater than mankind. Does it answer prayers? Perhaps. When I asked for help, help came. Is there a Christian God of heaven and hell? I'm not sure, but I know that there is something beyond this life and death, something different from what most of us are taught to expect. The unseen but felt presence when Dad was ill reinforced my sense of a power greater than myself. What Ruth shared about her out-of-body experiences in the hospital when doctors had pronounced her dead leaves me wondering. She described leaving her body, hovering close to the ceiling, and hearing the doctors pronounce her dead. Someone, or something, told her that it was not yet time, and she returned to her body. Traditional religious beliefs exclude so much of the mystery and mystical beliefs found in literature, legend, and fantasy that I have to believe there is something more. Individual powers, witchcraft, and the early knowledge of the Old Ones cannot be rationally explained away. Yet they are not all fairy tales, unless one believes that fairy tales derive from truth.

Experience also teaches about human emotions—love, despair, betrayal, anger, hurt, indifference, hope, joy, sorrow, and acceptance. It took me many years to work through these, and I'm not an expert with them yet. In looking back, I know that additional years have added insight, but I'm still learning.

Love has many faces: innocence, young love, romance, the reality of marriage, and the acceptance of another for what he is, not what you thought he was. There is love for a child, the protecting, the letting go, and the pride in growth and achievement.

Then, there is despair over love lost—the turning away from a loved one's indifference. The despair when Gerry was hospitalized—the utter emptiness, loss, betrayal, and anger when we were told that he was dead. Despair was the ache of empty arms when I could no longer hold him, the helplessness when my love was insufficient to heal him. Despair was the hurt of loss that I locked away and could not share. I felt that despair, frustration, and agony again when Deidre was ill in 1984—when doctors could not diagnose her illness but eventually put a tentative label of multiple sclerosis on her case. Worst of all was the helplessness, the denial from Bud instead of support and a sharing of grief, and then, the distancing. I felt myself to be totally alone in making decisions. Bud was in Portland with me for a while but returned to Idaho and work. I had Ruth, but at the bottom line, I was alone. Ruth could only lend a loving shoulder and advice. That is almost as lonely as the emptiness in my arms when I left Gerry behind that afternoon at the hospital. His brief stay taught me the importance of a child, and his passing revealed an ending that I would not see and accept.

Joy often comes tinged with the grey of uncertainty. I had been glad to discover that I was pregnant a second time, yet apprehensive that this child would also have problems. Joy was in the sense of triumph when Deidre was born and nothing was wrong. I felt joy as I watched her develop. This joy finally softened the sorrow of the earlier losses of Gerry, Koki, Dad, and Sheba.

Sorrow

Permit me to tell you about sorrow
For I carried my old cat, Sheba, to the vet,
Watched my father deteriorate and die,
Buried an infant son one snowy day,
And saw Dee hurting and wasting away
While I stood unable to help.
Yet the sorrow I hold within
Leaves me empty and alone
As you drive away
With our problems unsolved.

Presumption

You presume too much
When you expect
That I will live within your limits.
I'm not a trophy, nor a prize
To be won and then possessed.

The essence that is me
Suffocates,
Stultifies.

Having, owning is not the
Same as sharing, giving.

I must be free to give:
But to give, I must receive.
Love must be nurtured.
Without daily care it withers.
Like arid land
I await the rain,
The joy of another's caring.

Journal Entry, 1986

In the two years since Deidre was ill and I collapsed, my nerves have healed and the hypoglycemia is under control. Still, there is an emotional gap. I lack trust in others. I can count on me when the chips are down, but Bud is not there when I need him. That taints my feelings for him. I have created emotional barriers for protection, but I cannot love without also feeling respect, and that is gone. This makes for hard going now that he is home on a regular basis. I feel alienated, separate, and resentful of his interference in my daily life and routine. I am not eager to share my ideas with him. He puts me down too often with, "You always want to argue."

On the surface, we have everything two people could want—a lovely daughter, a nice home, cars paid for, a house filled with antiques, our health, work, and outside interests—everything to make life a success. Nevertheless, for me, there is a hollow core, an emptiness in my life. I yearn for a complete relationship with understanding, companionship, and intimacy, but for now, I settle for less. For years, I thought my life would be better if Bud were home. Now, that isn't at all true. I have learned to be alone or separate, and I am finding it very hard to give up that autonomy. I like me better when I am alone. There is less tension.

I fill my time with research, books, and writing. My

poetry has been published in *These Too Shall Be Heard*, volumes I and II, *Oregon English*, and *Words on the Wind*. I am not unhappy, but I wouldn't say my life is filled with joy or a zest for living. There is a sense of waiting for something to happen or for someone to come. Why don't I make a change? To what? I am not so dissatisfied that I want to throw away all that I have in order to begin again. Granted, time passes and I grow older, not younger. Change is never easy, and it will probably get harder. There's always an if! Perhaps I'm too comfortable the way I am. At any rate, I do not seek ways to create a change.

Of Me

How much of me do I define with things?
A home…warm…open
filled with treasures of my life
furnishings of dark solid wood…
fabrics, some muted, others rich
vibrant with color…
glass, warm in the light
or translucent
or sparkling…
dolls
music and books
plants…

How much of me is part of you?
A difficult birth…
Shared loss of a son.
A daughter, blue-eyed
who wrapped you 'round
her tiny finger from day one.
A home we built,
and sold because
I wanted a new career.
Sometime laughter…
Muted joys…
The trips to the coast
Walks on the beach
(even though you preferred to stay inside.)
The antique auctions…
delight of a new find
headiness of taking the bid
of spending…
How much of me is…

protective coloration…
shared events…
mutual goals?

How much of me
has no part of you
or the trappings of our life?
How much of me is within
the dampered emotions beneath,
controlled, efficient…
a fault line under the mask
the latent artist
who sees canvas, colors,
connections
the almost writer
who gropes for
something to say
a way to commit, to begin
a novel waiting to be born.
the once musician
who itches to play
but with fingers stiff
from lack of practice
listens instead.
the avid reader
who thinks about writing,
debates about painting,
who is frustrated with sewing
or gardening
or teaching
who indulges
fills shelves with favorites
can't pass up a bookstore
builds stacks on the floor.
How much of me is only a dreamer
who wishes for

that one golden moment
who climbs the mountain
only to see a higher peak beyond.

How much of me is all of these?
I'm like a puzzle:
Take away a single piece
I'm incomplete.

**

The child in me loves bright colors—the reds and gold of autumn leaves. She loves to scuff her feet through fallen leaves, tilt her head, and lean into the wind. The child in me likes to snuggle deeper under covers when cold morning dawns. She likes a furry robe and a comfy chair. She likes to sit and sip a hot drink while the fireplace warms the room.

The child in me requires solitude and space. Bright lights and loud noises irritate and are offensive. Quiet music soothes her; the outdoors calms her jangled nerves. Growing is hard work for the inner child who needs time to assimilate and make the world her own. In a world where privacy is difficult, she retreats into an inner sanctuary—a book, a pen, or a mood. Only then can she achieve understanding of all that she has observed.

The child in me wants to be held, to be cared for. She is tired of standing alone even though she has worked hard to gain a sense of identity and independence. This child can be perverse and hard to live with because she is moody, hard to satisfy, and feels deprived, neglected, or alone.

**

As days grew shorter in the fall of 1987 driving to work in Klamath Falls put me out of the house before daylight. Some mornings I watched the sun rise over the hills to the east. Some mornings I drove in rain or falling snow. Even in the short, five-minute drive, I was exposed to the elements and nature's ever-changing scene.

From the Classroom Window

Spray swirls and fogs
Thrown upward by spinning tires.
A wet orange sphere
Rests drunkenly upon the field;
Evidence of children gone from play.

Wet black fingers of an apple tree
Point skyward, thin clad
By slick brown leaves
Hesitating—shaken by sudden wind;
Waiting the sudden tumble
And the trampling underfoot.

Olene Gap at Dawn

Day wakes alone.
She thrusts her tousled head
Above enfolding hills,
Glints through one bright eye
Half hidden behind a lock of grey;

Then, as if decision made,
She brightens.
The luminescent east
Gives way to blue.
Her eye reddened by morning smoke
Clears to a silvery gleam.
Enshrouding darkness gives way
As she spreads her mantle
Of autumn scarlet and gold.

My Year-Long Christmas

Cotton white obscures the street
As fog enshrouds the day.
Snow glazes the ground;
Jack Frost bedecks bare branches;
December is here again.

It's time to cut and trim a tree,
Shop madly for that just-right gift,
Wrap packages in bright paper, and
Write messages to send afar.

It's time to remember the year soon past:
A weeklong writing workshop
At Lewis and Clark
Time of renewal, retreat, a boon.
A mad trip to northern Idaho
To obtain a purple plate, carnival glass,
A rainbow of light, wishbone and spades;
Then back to Oregon and down the West Coast,
Always searching…

The quest ending at Pistol River
Where giant spruces, alders, and two palms,
Sand and waves and rocks create
A site to build upon.

Tucked in between, I found:
   A visit with Ruth,
   New finds in genealogy,
   New books,
   Cemetery transcriptions,
   Teddy Bears!
   Dee in SCA with wizards and dragons
   Bud, unemployed and home
(Yard work, home repairs, new upholstery)
All this and more:
   Thanksgiving in Stockton, California,
   Glass shows at Modesto and Chico,
   Crafts Fair at Orland (I found a mule).

Santa needn't come at Christmas:
He's been here all year!

Things Worth Trying

I try to keep a straight face
Or draw a straight line
But never succeed.
A chuckle breaks through,
The line wavers.

I'll try to bake a decadence cake
Full of chocolate and nuts.
Then I'll try to eat just one bite.

I try to shave calories
To save for a treat.
I try to slim inches,
But bow to defeat.

To solve a puzzle
To win a car
To live
relax
enjoy.

Journal entry, January 28, 1987

The ever-changing view from my classroom window differs again today. Late last night, wet ploppy flakes of snow covered everything. Now, the morning sun in the east glistens on the snow-wrapped lines and limbs across the way. A single arrow of white plummets to the ground as ice releases its grip on an overhead cable. White-latticed cyclone fencing in the foreground forms a stiff border around the schoolyard. Beyond, no mountains or hills march into the distance. All is soft haze rising into the steel-blue grey of dense clouds.

**

Last Summer

Last summer I did not write a book, but I took a writing workshop. I did not travel to Iowa, Missouri, or New York, but I did make a flying visit through northeast Oregon to northern Idaho and then to Portland, to Seaside, and then south along the Oregon coast.

Last summer I did not paint a picture or write a symphony. I cleaned the house and mowed the lawn. I did not solve my genealogy snags, but I acquired new material on one family line. I did not order microfilm, but I spent many hours in the library.

Poetry

Words sparking pictures
A tune in my head
A single droplet
of rain hanging
on a green leaf edge
Rain thundering
on a metal roof
An ache deep inside
that won't be eased
A yearning toward precision
the exactness
of the mathematician
Poetry is life.

Chapter 11: Dying Embers

Loner

Once open and giving,
A giver
Taken
Hurt
Rejected.

Protective walls
To hide behind;
A shield against
barbs and innuendoes;
A moat for distance
A quiet demeanor
That belies the hurt.

Fragile walls built
Day by day
Stone by stone
Word by word...
Insulating
Protecting
Isolating.

Walls that shelter...
Walls that cage...
The once-open spirit
Now longs to break free.

**

Risking

I filled each day, one after the other, with classes and students, as we learned to write together and explored new textbooks before selecting one to adopt. At times, I filled the empty spaces with typing and proofing the manuscript for the cemetery book.

One such morning before class began and as I was setting up the film projector, an arm came from behind, turned me around into an embrace. As his lips came down to mine, I hesitated. Should I? Or should I turn my head away? The old tapes in my head said "No!" But I turned a deaf ear and responded. Could I feel again?

Yes! Oh, yes! Ice no longer wrapped my heart, and the granite walls, erected with painstaking care, cracked. He was not my husband; he was just a friend reaching out for affirmation in his pain. He cared but not enough, yet in the brief flurry of our sharing, I learned to take a chance with life once more.

I Remember

Rain pounding on the roof
in time with strong piano chords.

I remember one clear droplet
hanging from a green tooth-edged leaf.

I remember sunlight
through tall redwoods
spotlighting a single fern,
forming a fairy stairway
rising to the sky.

I remember daffodils
like fresh butter
nodding beside the road.

I remember the blue-green waves
curling, breaking
churning into foam
against black rocks, and then,
flashing away in spray.

I remember footprints
ovals in the sand,
your bigger track
ahead of mine.
But most of all, I remember
separateness,
two alone, even
when together.

Dragons of the Mind

The path to the beach is open. Deer have used it, and horses have left their imprint. A haze of fog and perhaps smoke swathes the day in grey. The air is cool, not really misty but certainly not dry.

Today is a day of solitude, it seems. Although the neighbors had lights last night, I've seen no one today. Two small families explored the beach—and one lonely seagull—each keeping to himself. I wandered for an hour my leg muscles pulling from the sand, taking pictures, and watching waves. Now I sit with my back to the window but with a roar filling my ears. It pervades my senses and establishes its own rhythm within me.

Our relationship lies tangled between us, knotted tightly like pink yarn around a playful puppy—each tight knot a problem to be solved; each strand a memory to bind us. Memories like instant glue keep us together. I write volumes, and you live on the telephone, trying to consume the miles between us. Worry and weariness weight your voice. I feel the heaviness across the miles, carried by invisible signals—telepathy of machines conveying each shade of emotion.

To concentrate on my inner turmoil is impossible. My thoughts are not centering. It is as if a physical need is exerting itself—a need to merge with the rhythm of the waves and to establish a different pace than the one I follow. Is that where I'm heading? A different lifestyle? A different drummer's beat? It feels right to verbalize these thoughts. A gull's cry echoes as if in affirmation.

Yellow leaves are on the willow near the bamboo grass, and the ivy has that sickly yellow-green look of fall. Sweet peas still form a riot of pink across the slopes, and the whites and yellows of wild flowers interlace the waving fronds of dried grasses and the rust of ironweed.

"I won't need you any more," wails the radio, but my heart disagrees. If I don't love you, why do I still include you in everything I do? So much of my life— twenty-eight years—is intertwined with yours. "I don't care if I'm not the first love you've known…as long as I'm the last." I must learn to trust, and that's hard. How do I erase the scars of past pain—forgiven but never forgotten—like surgery, always the scar to remind me of the hurt? How do we rebuild what I've lost or let wander astray? Or do we simply begin in a new place and time like two strangers who meet?

Two lonely people
Living side by side
Never share:
Speak only trivialities.

Hugs become infrequent
Kisses lack fire.

Warmth is allowed to cool;
Love's fire sinks into ashes.

You go your way;
I go mine.
We hurt inside
But never tell.

The dragons of the mind are unpredictable and frightening. Old memories and tapes, they continue to influence even when I am unaware of their presence. The old *shoulds* and *should nots* from my youth create guilt in the present. They give me self-doubt when I try to act on my intuition. I vacillate between *maybe* and *if,* torn between hurting another and being hurt myself. As I hesitate, actions become reactions.

Dragons lure with material security and sameness; they make it easier to walk a safe road of habit than dare to risk that which I most desire. Dragons create in me a stranger, make me fear as a writer, yet I must dare the risk to rebuild my life and to write.

September Morn

A meadowlark shouted his joy;
I felt it ripple, rebound
Deep within me.
Liquid notes
no tinkle of breeze against chimes
no sob of wind through pines.
Echoes dropped, melted
became one
Clear dewdrop
Trembling on a pink rose petal.
A promise
of new day, new beginning
a more aware *me*.

Morning Rain

Pink blush stains the eastern sky.
Cottony fog swaddles Hogback.
The air is damp.
Fine mist on my shoulders
Becomes
Rain.

Grey lowering galleons
Sweep away the pink,
Rinse the air of dust,
Polish leaves etched with grime,
Bringing freshness
To parched soil,
One last burst of color
To late roses,
A bloom of yellow
For tomorrow's leaves.
Fall has arrived.

First Snow

Huge white plops of moisture
Upon the windshield
Chase away
Persistent rain.

Lovely to watch
Graceful in their descent,
Harbingers of cold winter's chill.

For an instant, they form patterns
Upon grey wool;
Another breath
And I drip unwanted water.

No, not fluffy blankets
To warm the earth;
Only penetrating damp
To be shed at first chance.

In the fall of 1987, Bud left to work as a supervisor for the remodeling of a coal generation plant in Pennsylvania, Deidre was a sophomore in high school, and I went back to classes at Brixner. I was glad when he went, as I was more and more uncomfortable with his being home. I simply did not know what it was I wanted. I had no one to take his place, and I didn't know what I could do other than to teach.

This particular job was a management position for him, the best money that he had made in his career. He complained of the lack of men, the working conditions, and the weather. Still, he seemed to cope, and in some measure to find enjoyment in what he was doing. He asked me to fly there for the Thanksgiving break to see if there was anything left between us, upon which we could rebuild. Deidre at age sixteen was quite happy to stay with her aunt Carol.

My Bear

The bear in my life is not
A cuddly teddy bear. Instead,
He leads a solitary life
Away from me
Grubbing his sustenance
From Pennsylvania coalfields.
Like the bear,
He is shaggy in winter
With grey hair grown long
And a beard that furs and warms his face.
Wrapped in layers
Of insulating clothing
Under a bulky coat,
He resembles the portly bear who
Waddles into winter.
In manner, too,
He becomes bearish,
Growling his discontent with his world.
He withdraws to his lair
To nurse his woes
Before foraging anew for another day.

I flew out of Klamath Falls to San Francisco, where I enplaned for Chicago and then for Harrisburg, Pennsylvania, where Bud was to meet me. I did not know to use the shuttle in San Francisco and missed the boarding call for my flight. Eventually, I was allowed to board in place of someone who was on call for a chance seat. I learned that nylons and heels are not the footwear for traveling; they did not allow me to move quickly over long concourses.

The stop at O'Hare airport in Chicago was just that, a stop. The city lights shone brightly as seen from the air, but on the ground, I saw nothing more exciting than more people. Fortunately, the transfer was not complicated this time, and I once again found myself airborne for the last short flight to Harrisburg. There I arrived on time, but my luggage did not arrive until the next day. I had a carry-on bag of essentials that got me through until my bags were delivered to Shenandoah the next day. I had a problem with the local pronunciation of "Shen-doh."

We spent a busy four days sightseeing. I wanted to go to Philadelphia and Gettysburg, but distances made that impractical. Instead, I saw the surrounding local area. We drove to Lancaster for an auction where as much German as English was spoken. The Pocono Mountains, highest in that area, were unimpressive hills without snow, though they are noted for their skiing. As this was a deciduous tree area, the slopes wore bare limbs as winter attire. The architecture impressed me far more than anything else did. Every village seemed to have several churches, and not all of them were small and plain. Some were Greek or Russian Orthodox, and had onion-ball towers with gilded paint, as if they had been transported intact from Russia. I saw brick and frame construction. Row houses of both types were evident, even in Shenandoah, where the rows followed the contour of the land, each unit stepping up or down as the slope demanded.

We spent one day shopping in Reading, Pennsylvania, at the outlet stores—a new shopping concept for me. I was familiar with Lloyd Center in Portland, or Washington Square near Tigard, but neither of these prepared me for Reading, where entire buildings were outlets for manufacturing companies. Merchandise was perhaps flawed in some minor way, yet the items I looked over were fine and reasonably priced. I bought tights and outfits for aerobics class, a new wool coat at Burlington, fabric for Deidre's prom dress and the skirt that I wore at her wedding, and two other pieces that went into a trunk. I bought a magenta-colored knit hat, and a stuffed raccoon with huge eyes and a ringed tail. At a flea market, I found Christmas ornaments created out of harness bells, ribbon, and roses. One of these later became a model for my own creations.

Life wasn't perfect, yet there were still things Bud and I enjoyed doing together. Bud suggested that I quit teaching, as his earnings were sufficient to make this possible. When I returned to Klamath Falls, I applied for a sabbatical for the following year but did not get it. I put the house on the market, thinking that with a depressed housing market it would no doubt take all winter to find a buyer. To my surprise, a couple from California liked the house and wished to move in as soon as possible. Bud flew home for Christmas, and we went house hunting for a rental. The closest one in the suburbs near Brixner was not the worst, by any means, but it really wasn't what I wanted. Finally, we widened our search to the city proper and found a small two-bedroom house located on Darrow Street. This was a house that I felt Deidre could handle as she finished her last year of high school. The much smaller size of the house meant that most of the household furnishings and antiques would go into storage at Union.

Ask Me

When the boxes are all packed,
The decisions made, ask me
Why I worked so long
For what I didn't need.
I look at rosewood, oak, and walnut,
Gloat over Zolan plates and Japanese dolls.
I treasure the Kestners and Heubach.
The Gulick and Remington are my delight.
The Silver Ghost was the final fillip
On the cake.
How easily I pack them all away.
Ask me how and why.

Ask me what comes next.
I'll shrug.
To write, to paint, perhaps to school.
Who knows?
The inner drive is stronger
Than all our plans.
I'll shake my head and smile.
It is a necessary thing
I do,
Even to the unknowing.

By this time, my nerves had mostly healed. I coped with school and home, and even succeeded in planning the new schedule of classes for the 1988–89 school year. My mind worked again, even if emotions were still sometimes shaky.

With the thought of moving in mind, earlier in the fall I had begun packing antiques for storage at Union. Bud had left me the pickup, so I was able to cull from both the house and the garage. I removed two full loads before showing the house to the realtors.

The house always took hours to clean and dust, but until I removed all the excess and still could not see emptiness, I did not realize just how many items we had accumulated over a twenty-year period. I had taken two truckloads, yet the china cabinets were still well stocked, furniture was in place, statues and pictures still decorated the rooms, and the bookshelves were full. And I could see a difference between a comfortable home and one that had had the clutter of a not-too-well-managed museum.

Even with the furniture that I moved into storage—the walnut breakfront, the oak organ, the walnut dining set, the oak buffet, and the small china cabinet—there was still too much for the little rental house. The single-car garage became a storage unit for boxes and small things until weather was again open enough to move more things to Union. Deidre and I managed quite well in the smaller home, and I could see it as a home for her and her boyfriend Dennis when I joined Bud at his next job in Michigan. Bud was not happy with these plans, but he could do nothing. Both Deidre and Dennis were sure of themselves, but wanted time together before marrying. Knowing how my marriage had not worked, I could not say, "Marry first."

In the spring of 1988, I took a one-year, unpaid, leave of absence from Brixner Junior High, but I had no intention of returning. After eight years with seventh- and eighth-graders, I was burned out and needed a change. Before school was out, Bud sold his Honda Prelude and purchased a red Mazda RX-7, the sports car that he did not buy when my station wagon died. At the end of the last week of school, I flew into Hartford, Connecticut, to meet him. He had finished with his job a week earlier and had visited the New England area. Now I was to get a flying tour. He met me at the airport, made a quick trip back to the motel where he repacked my extra luggage with his surplus, and then delivered it back to the airport for the return flight to Klamath Falls where his sister would collect the bags the next day.

Anticipation filled me as we headed north through all the spring greenery of Vermont and New Hampshire. I wanted to see the land and places about which I had read so much. I remember lunching at a rustic place nestled in some trees beside the highway, and I think it was here that I bought the crystal globe that hung from the rearview mirror of the RX for eight years.

The road wound over and through the mountains, followed a winding river through the main part of one town, passed grey barns and Holstein cows, and finally dropped into Bar Harbor, Maine, with the grey Atlantic Ocean stretching like dull pewter to the east. The sunset over the harbor with windjammer masts etched in black against the sky made for a strong image, as did a boiled lobster dinner with all the trimmings. Here, I found a lavender and white afghan for Deidre.

From Bar Harbor, we headed southwest toward New York. As we traveled through New England, I recognized place names from my genealogy research, even though I had no material with me to help pin down who was where. Bud was in a hurry, though, so I could not prowl and was disappointed. In New York, we followed the Mohawk River and the Erie Canal and then, at my insistence, dropped one hundred miles south into the Finger Lakes region to visit Springwater where the Crandalls, Rues, and Browns had spent time during the 1840s. I wanted one chance to experience the geographic roots of my research. We stopped once in that area to browse through a lady's yard sale and came away with an art deco bronze lamp.

From Springwater, we traveled northwest to Niagara Falls, crossed into Canada, bypassed Toronto—a string of lights by night—and headed west toward Chicago. At Chicago, we turned north into Wisconsin, spent the night in a motel, and took a couple of hours to revisit

Beaver Dam, again finding the museum that contained models made by Uncle Herman Bramer. That museum also has the hand-carved cherry-wood rocker that he made for his wife Hulda and some early records of pioneers in Dodge County. I searched for headstones in St. Patrick's Cemetery but could not locate the one for George and Bridget Schoenberger. By this time, Bud was getting irritated and kept saying that he had to get home so he wouldn't miss a call from his company. I don't know why he didn't phone them, but he didn't. And the faster he drove, the more frustrated I became. Even with a stop for antiques at Tomah, Wisconsin, we made the return trip through the Bighorn Mountains and Yellowstone to Oregon in just under a week.

There had been no calls from his boss, and none came for almost two months. As he was still supposed to go to Michigan—no call had indicated otherwise—we shopped for a travel trailer that would be large enough to live in but small enough to tow easily with the Chevy pickup. We finally settled on a thirty-five-foot fifth-wheel Terry. I liked the living arrangement with blond wood and dusty rose upholstery. We bought it without furniture, which allowed me to use my loveseat, chair, corner table, and bed.

When the call came, the company asked Bud to go to South Carolina for thirty days on a nuclear plant job instead of to Michigan. He parked the trailer at Carol and Bill's place, left both vehicles, and flew south. I stayed in the trailer with Tiger. With one extension and then another, the thirty days actually became a six-month stretch. Tiger and I finally decided I'd join him in Augusta, Georgia, where he'd rented a one-bedroom apartment. The trailer and Chevy pickup would remain parked until the following summer.

On October 29, leaving Deidre with Dennis and my checkbook in Klamath Falls to finish her senior year, I got in the RX-7 and headed out on my first trip across country alone. I headed across the mountains to Lakeview and then south on Highway 140 along Parsnip Creek to Winnemucca, Nevada. I remember that instead of a DEER CROSSING sign along the highway, I saw a bright yellow OPEN RANGE sign adorned with a longhorn steer. After dinner in a casino—the best food in town, according to the motel manager—I spent the night in Winnemucca and was on the road before daylight. I watched the sun ascend over the salt flats east of Wendover, Nevada. Among the pictures in my head is one of Price Canyon, Utah—the highway winding along the river that ran between rock-strewn canyon walls with juniper trees growing where they found enough soil to put down roots.

I followed the Colorado River and passed through Boothill with its Tombstone Drive west of Montrose, Colorado. From Montrose, Highway 50 led into the Sangre de Cristo Mountains, and a mountain valley where sheep and llamas grazed. I followed the Arkansas

River with its bristlecone pines overhanging the water and saw early snow on the upper slopes of the Sangre de Cristos. I was crossing the land alone with no one to set the pace and no one to nag at me for running late. I started early or late and drove until I was tired. I stopped when I chose.

Royal Gorge National Park was a must. Dad had crossed here in 1928, and here I was, visiting in late 1988, sixty years later. The gorge and the bridge that crossed it had not changed from the pictures Dad had in his scrapbook. Several deer, including a large buck, were panhandling in the parking lot by the time I was ready to leave. I could not resist a few photos, probably the only close-up shot of a buck with a large rack that I'll ever take. I also recorded my presence in Bent County, where I captured in photos the sign at the county line, as well as a coyote mural done in small tiles, and cacti at the rest area. The Colorado–Kansas line was commemorated with a vivid sunset, and Dodge City by the moon.

I took the byways when possible to avoid traffic and because I wanted to see the fall colors. Highway 77 south to Winfield, Kansas, took me through farm country with its red barns and scarlet maples. The oaks were still green but turning. To my delight, I saw my first longhorns close to the highway. That meant another photo opportunity. Before I left Missouri to cross the Mississippi River, I finally saw cotton in a field east of Dexter, Missouri. Granted, the harvest was finished, but I could still see white tufts hanging tightly to brown stalks. Crossing the river into Kentucky, I wanted to stop, but the bridge was narrow and no pull-offs were available on the bridge or on either side.

I was heading to Somerset, Kentucky, which according to the map was approximately one hundred fifty miles by toll road, but because it was a shorter, more scenic route, I chose a narrow highway that wound along beneath overhanging green trees. What the map did not show were the ups, downs, and arounds that the road took as it followed the contours of the Kentucky hills. Once, I found myself behind a piece of farm equipment with no room to pass. I passed through Fancy Farm, Kentucky, where St. Jerome Church dominated the town square. The highway stopped at the church then made an abrupt right turn around the square. Just as the sun was setting, I reached Land Between the Lakes and the entrance to Golden Pond.

The next morning was misty with rain. I passed by a log cabin on the campus of West Kentucky State University in Bowling Green, and then found myself in Pulaski County, where I saw tobacco hanging to dry in a barn.

In Somerset, I stopped to ask questions and try to find additional material on the Stephens family who had lived in this area. The only definite data was the same marriage information that I had already acquired.

Outside of Somerset, I discovered that Fishing Creek was wider, deeper, and greener than many of Oregon's rivers. From Somerset, I headed south, and a thunderstorm caught up with me at the Grave Hill United Baptist Church.

Roll of Thunder

Towering white clouds build
one upon the other
Crowding
Shoving
Absorbing moisture
Darkening

Heads bump
A rumble of ancient drums
Sounds in the distance
Carried faintly on the rising wind
Soaring
Swirling
Tossing my hair
as I halt and watch
the jagged lightning flash

The drums roll
Recalling men at war
In a world dark with hatred
Another flash
The roll becomes a howl
Rain cleanses the earth;
Emotions purge the soul.

Stopping to photograph tobacco hanging in a Tennessee barn, I followed the Appalachian Highway south toward Asheville, North Carolina, and Georgia. I made a stop in Neel's Gap, Georgia, to purchase two tall pottery mugs, and enjoy the reds and golds of leaves against the rugged bluffs of the Appalachians. Everyone told me that the fall leaves had passed their peak of brilliance, yet I still found a glorious riot of leaves still hanging tightly to limbs while those that had fallen flamed anew with every swirl of errant breeze.

I arrived in Augusta to find the weather in Georgia far milder than the snow and cold of the Klamath Basin and the high desert region I knew. It was November, but lawns retained their green, and late flowers still bloomed. Because of higher humidity, I was happy to have an air conditioner. Most times, I was comfortable in blouses or a light jacket while native Augustans wore coats. During the week while Bud worked, I spent time in Augusta City Library dredging for the gold of historical facts. I found *Dormant Peerages*, which added to numerous British lines. I also found Quaker records for Wrightsboro that provided more material on my Scott ancestors, including immigration information from Scotland for the immigrant Scott. At the genealogical society, I found the Wurts's multivolume work, *Magna Charta Sureties*. This, too, traced and documented British lines.

Augusta College Library, with its room for holdings

of the historical society, was my favorite. Here, among other things, I found Ohio Bible records for the Kerr family. I often spent four or five hours digging through books before I would head home to fix a meal. I took two notebooks with me to Augusta, but when it was time to return to Oregon, I shipped four file-boxes of copied materials that I had gathered. My winter of research provided raw material for future work.

On weekends and when Bud had time, we explored. Again, I discovered geographic names that echoed my Quaker research as we crossed South Carolina to visit Charleston. I fell in love with the houses, the cobbled alleys, and the whole feel of that city. I cannot say the same for Savannah, where shaggy moss hung like straggly hair from branches of sprawling trees. The resonance was not that of Charleston. I bought a small trunk at a flea market in the Atlanta area and visited Stone Mountain, which to me was no grander than an ordinary eastern Oregon hill.

When we left the Augusta airport to fly west to spend Christmas with Deidre, pansies were blooming amid a light fall of snow. Later in the day, that snowfall blanketed the Appalachians and closed the airports. We landed in Klamath Falls to find six to eight inches on the ground there. Dennis was in Australia enjoying a trip with his parents and brother. This was the last Christmas the three of us would spend alone together.

When I joined Bud in Georgia, I had nurtured a

fading hope that we could renew our marriage. It didn't happen. We shared the small apartment like roommates—both gone during the day to our separate interests. Television dominated the evenings as I knit a sweater, quilted a baby quilt, or culled my notes from the day's research at the library. We spent weekends exploring the countryside. I saw other road signs naming places from my research and gathered dry data from books, but was unable to revive the corpse of our relationship.

Before we left Georgia for good in late March 1989, we visited Andersonville National Cemetery. By then the redbuds and dogwoods were blooming. Had I known, I could have looked up information on Civil War burials for some of our family, but I did not make these connections until later. When we finally headed back to Oregon across the lower states, we dropped south from Augusta to the Florida coast before turning west to Pensacola. The sands were white with grey-green grass softening the beaches along Chatawahatchee Bay. The aqua water of the Gulf of Mexico was not at all like the greens of the Pacific along the Oregon Coast, nor was it the blue-grey of the Northern Atlantic.

I had wanted to visit New Orleans before leaving the South; however, that was not meant to be. Instead, we turned north to visit Vicksburg Battlefield before turning west across northern Louisiana. As I walked through Vicksburg, the scars of battle in cannon-blasted trees, breastworks, and trenches were still visible, although time had softened the edges with moss and shrubbery. With eyes closed and a little effort, it was not hard to hear the boom of cannons or the crackle of artillery fire.

Vicksburg

Shattered trees
With broken limbs like arms
And legs strewn across the pockmarked
Ground,
Open, unhealed wounds upon the earth,
Grim reminders of arcing cannon balls
Fallen coursers
Dying men.

Like scattered drops of blood
Against new green,
An early redbud blooms
Against the hundred-year-old scars.

There was little of interest to me in Louisiana, Oklahoma, or across northern Texas. In Tucumcari, New Mexico, we purchased some Indian pottery for Deidre. We passed through Flagstaff, Arizona, and reached the Grand Canyon late in the day, just as the tourist center was closing. Still, we were able to walk a small portion of the rim, and I obtained one of my best photos—the canyon framed in the V of a juniper tree. Later, we crossed the desert into southern California before again turning north. That was a desert of sand and cactus, not of sage or juniper. The Joshua trees are like nothing we have in eastern Oregon.

Back in Klamath Falls, even as Deidre completed her senior year at Mazama High School, she and Dennis were planning an SCA wedding with appropriate medieval garb and had set the date for May 26, 1990. By that time, Deidre would have finished one year at Willamette University. Thus, I spent my time between April and June selecting fabrics and sewing wedding garments. Deidre's outer dress and Den's *cote hardi*—a snug, tunic jacket with close-fitting sleeves and a dagged, or pointed, lower edge that just covered his hips—as well as a bishop's robe were to be of white velvet. We selected white satin for her dress, black satin for Gerry's tunic and April's skirt (Den's parents), and blue satin for Bud's tunic. I already had a dark blue satin for my skirt. The robe, skirts, and tunics were to be banded with three-inch picot-edged satin ribbon and appliquéd with silk featherstitching and pearls. The bishop's robe was lined with red satin and banded in red; the black tunic and skirt were both banded in red; the blue tunic had white bands, and the blue skirt was finished with cream.

By June 1989 and graduation, Deidre had received her acceptance from Willamette University in Salem and was to enter the fall of 1989. Bud remained in Oregon, between the Georgia and Michigan jobs, just long enough for us to locate a house for her. She needed housing suitable for a cat and a boyfriend that would not fit into the freshman dorm housing. After searching real-estate flyers and repossessed homes held by the Veteran's Administration, we found one that was livable, though it needed substantial work. It was also close to the university.

Most of our household things had already gone into storage, but I had kept the baby grand piano and large curved-front china cabinet. I hated to let the piano go, but the Salem house had no room for it. I enjoyed it but didn't live for music, and Deidre didn't play at all. Therefore, I sold it. Once graduation was over, Dennis, Deidre, and I sorted a load and moved it to Union for storage. The next step was to get the Salem house ready to occupy. That took both cleaning and painting. The main floor had hardwood flooring hidden beneath worn carpet, while the upstairs had new carpet. We tore up carpeting, refinished floors, painted ceilings and walls, and hung new blinds and curtains.

Each time we drove from Klamath Falls to Salem, a load of things went with us. That left the rental to clean and the final loads to move. Dennis loaded his Camaro and towed his sailboat; Deidre filled her little car with the fragile items and her Shadow cat; and I drove the loaded Chevy pickup, towing a trailer filled with appliances and other items. Driving the pickup with its stick shift on the floor was not easy for me, and I had never towed a trailer. My legs seemed too short to reach the clutch and my right arm was never long enough to reach the angle of the gearshift. Worse yet, we left Klamath Falls late enough in the day that we would reach Salem after dark—and I was driving blind, as the trailer was too wide for me to see with side mirrors. The Santiam Pass was a nightmare, but I geared down and felt as if I was creeping down the western grade. We finally arrived safely in Salem with no mishaps.

I stayed in Salem long enough to help get the house settled. By then, Bud had located a place for the fifth-wheel trailer and had it towed to Michigan. I had packed the trailer and sent it off before leaving Klamath Falls. That left only Tiger and my personal things to move. By then we were into July, and summer heat was climbing. I stopped in the Tri-Cities area of southern Washington to purchase a harness for Tiger. He wore a collar and handled well on a leash, but I felt more secure with a harness. He didn't mind it either; in fact, I think he had more freedom with it than with the collar. He expected that I would stop so that he could walk and explore. He did let me know, though, that the air conditioner was a necessity. If I stopped for gas and the cab began to warm up, he'd meow at me until I had the air back on. Then he'd settle on his perch on top of the cooler where he had a breeze in his face and surround-vision. To secure him, I seat-belted the cooler and padded the top for him.

This trip doesn't stand out as eventful. We just tried to stay cool. At one stop in Montana, I did discover that even if I knew how to add oil to the pickup, there was no way that I could, short of climbing up under the hood. I was just too short. Eventually, I followed Interstate 90, went north through Fargo, North Dakota, across Minnesota and Wisconsin, and entered Michigan just west of Iron Mountain.

That winter of 1989–90, I subbed in area schools around Iron Mountain, just north of the Wisconsin border. I could have kept quite busy because I was one of the few teachers who would accept a seventh-and eighth-grade assignment. However, it did not take me long to decide that if I was teaching, I wanted to be in charge. I was not comfortable with dropping in for a day at a time. However, I did enjoy the little boy that I tutored in reading at his home twice a week. Besides subbing, I pursued my research in Escanaba's libraries. Resources were not as plentiful as those I had found in Georgia, but I read many microfilms at the family history center. That winter saw four to five feet of snow piled along our driveway, with at least eighteen inches on ground and at times more than that, I think. There was no need for the team and sleigh that Dad remembered from his youth—once you cleared your driveway, the roads were open because the highway department used a salt mixture to keep the asphalt ice-free. This is very hard on the vehicles, though. They show rust within a couple winters of use there; however, getting from one place to another is done with ease.

That winter, I drove to Escanaba once a week to use the research facilities. The state library archive branch was located about one block from the shore of Green Bay, which opened into Lake Michigan. I would arrive there by eight o'clock in the morning in order to spend a full day with the books. The street was a white glitter of packed snow and ice that melded into the snow packs on the bay—it was hard to tell where land and water met. At that time of morning, streetlights still lit the fog or mist, and the sky was a steel-grey curtain meeting the snow.

On weekends, Bud and I went south to Green Bay to shop. On our return late one afternoon, I got my first look at the northern lights—a fantasy of dancing light almost unseen, yet there, glimpsed from the corner of the eye but gone when viewed straight on. When the weather broke in the spring, we explored the various roads within a day's drive. We attended a few auctions, drove to Lake Superior, and visited Door County.

If I wasn't researching, tutoring, or sightseeing, I spent time walking or sewing. That winter I made a wall quilt of velvet and satin, sewed spandex tights and velvet codpieces for Dennis for Christmas, created memento wreath pillows, and then began again on wedding attire. Dennis constructed his *cote hardi*, and I did all the silver thread/pearl embroidery work. Then I made Deidre's veil and a hat for Bud.

In April, Tiger and I returned to Oregon, this time driving the RX-7, to begin sewing in earnest on Deidre's gown. Dennis did the designs and fitting while I tackled the machine work. In addition, he had made her a dark green velvet overdress and wanted to surprise her with an underdress to wear with it. Together, we made one of rose satin. Finally, all the sewing was finished—all we had left to do was hope for good weather because it usually rained Memorial Day weekend.

**

Fairy Tale Wedding

The princess in her castle dreams of a knight in shining armor who will carry her away to live happily ever after. In the mundane—or as most of us know it, the real world—this seldom happens. Yet on occasion, fantasy overlays reality to create something neither one nor the other. Careful planning created just such a moment on May 26, 1990, when Deidre married

Dennis Denham. In Society for Creative Anachronism (SCA) terms, Kathleen O'Shaunessy wed Dennis of Maplewood at the 1990 Egil's Tourney held at Fernridge Reservoir near Eugene, Oregon.

The morning dawned without rain, promising dry skies for the outdoor ceremony. As Dennis had set up the pavilion and established camp the previous day, little remained to be done except to assemble the wedding party and guests. Before the ceremony, a trio of Picts, painted in blue woad, stopped by to view the bride.

Deidre glowed with joy, every inch a princess in her white satin and velvet, her tulle veil secured by a coronet of roses and baby's breath. Dennis, her dark-haired Prince Charming in white velvet with silken tights, wore a sword at his side as he paced nervously. His brother Don, wearing leather armor and carrying a broad axe, stood at his side, while Deidre's matron of honor, Lady Zenobia in her wheelchair, wore a horned headdress. The minister, a woman and close friend of Deidre's from college, wore the white woolen alb of her faith beneath the velvet bishop's robe that I had made. Both fathers stood resplendent in satin tunics over dark pants, while the mothers, April and I, wore dark satin skirts and long-sleeved blouses—close enough to pass for period attire.

Dennis cut the wedding cake with his sword while Don threatened it with his axe. Guests helped themselves to cake with punch or black-cherry wine made from cherries picked the year Deidre was born. I had bottled the wine and stored it carefully for eighteen years to preserve its potency and bouquet. Without a doubt, it was a major hit with those who enjoyed wine. The rain held off until after the ceremony, but it did rain them out that night, and they headed back to Salem and their own home.

**

Bud had flown to Oregon for the wedding, but had to return to Michigan to finalize his job. As we still did not know where the next job would take him, I remained in Oregon. My father had died in 1985 but Mother still lived. However, her life was filled with an adopted son, Gary, and his friends. She was unable to attend the wedding and family relations were strained. Because I felt that the kids needed time alone, I took this chance to visit Ruth in Portland. We had not been able to spend much time together, so this gave us a chance to research together and to visit. We also took the opportunity to return to eastern Oregon and revisit Heppner, Hardman, the Independent Order of Odd Fellows (I.O.O.F.) Cemetery at Hardman, and the ranch near Top. On our way back to Portland, we detoured from Highway 97 to locate a cemetery in Wasco County. Here we found the grave of Hannah (Roth) Rue, wife of Schuyler Rue, our great-great grandfather who was buried in Linkville Cemetery in

Klamath Falls. It was different traveling with Ruth than with Bud or by myself. The tension and irritation that I felt with Bud was replaced by a sense of anticipation and sharing. Her memories of places added to mine, gave us both new insights.

Kingsley Cemetery

A tilted grey stone
Surrounded by
Summer's grass, a
Brown, tangled surf
Of a fossilized sea…
Shields
Mysteries,
Memories,
Lies.

Real secrets are buried:
Ghosts speak the truth.

By August, Bud was still in Michigan, and I had worn out my welcome with Ruth and Gary. No matter how well we got along, after a while, enough was enough. I packed my research papers, art supplies, and new paintings—the best that I have ever created—and returned to the kids in Salem. By the end of September, I was working part time at JoAnn Fabrics, and Bud had returned from Michigan without a job. The company that had employed him sold out and new management downsized supervisory personnel.

We parked the fifth-wheel trailer in the backyard of the Salem house, and there were now four of us with Tiger and Shadow in residence. Bud had withdrawn his 401K monies to supplement what I earned and did not seem to be in any hurry to locate new work. That winter I made jointed teddy bears, muslin dolls, and lambs for Made in Oregon and Made in Salem shops, Bazaar Mania, and as custom orders. Before I burned out crafting, I had shipped six dozen bears and twelve dozen small dolls dressed in Pendleton wool and had lost count of the lambs, pigs, and dolls that went through the bazaar and other outlets. Through this experience, I learned that no matter how much I enjoyed working with fabrics, there was no way I could create enough items fast enough to make this pay as a business. I hand-sewed leather toes, paws, and noses onto each bear, and embroidered the doll faces and lamb noses. I was creating art, not mass-production, and art is not profitable when it comes to crafting.

Over the next year, I continued to sell fabric and keep up with my crafts; Bud returned to the carpenters' union for intermittent work; and both Deidre and Dennis were in college. We managed to muddle along, although it was not always easy. We fell further and further behind financially.

In August of 1991, I began work as a library tech for Kerr Library at Oregon State University in Corvallis. This was an eighty-mile commute every day; however, I was able to work a ten-to-seven schedule and missed most of the commuter traffic. The added benefit of research facilities and reduced tuition offset the driving. I ordered all of the 1850 census film for the state of New York and took two classes in library science at Western Oregon State College while working at OSU. I used the computer to write my papers for these classes and learned to compose on the computer. For me, this was an entirely new concept in writing.

As a library tech, my job priority was to shelve all of the periodicals and journals. When that was finished, I shelved books, shelf-read, straightened shelves, and found books related to my research and interests. Each day found me collecting periodicals on the main floor and moving them to the fourth for sorting. From there, I shelved them in the current periodical reading area and then to each floor where back issues were shelved. I was responsible for the stacks on fourth floor. Each day I tried to walk the floor to maintain its appearance.

When I had completely shelf-read and straightened this floor, I moved my efforts to another. Students would pull books from shelves and leave them on reading tables. This was never a problem, because we knew they needed to be replaced. Problems occurred when books were misplaced on shelves or carried to another shelf and left lying where no one would think to look for them. I had never realized just how careless people could be when they browse for books, but I learned.

Chapter 12: Endings

While Bud was working on the construction of one of the new state buildings in November of 1991, he developed a hernia from lifting a sheet of plywood. This sent him to the hospital for surgery and then home for recovery through the winter. Without his income, my wages just didn't stretch far enough. I was about $400 short of meeting expenses each month.

I had expected Bud to find another job by spring, but he consigned antiques in an antique mall and began to frequent the flea markets instead. I liked fabric sales and my work at Kerr Library, but I saw that if I ever wanted financial security, I would have to provide it for myself. That meant a return to the classroom. I felt betrayed at that point, because I did not want to return to teaching.

Broken Promises

Promises like shattered crystal
Crunch beneath the heel of time.
The words once spoken, hang
Within the canyons of my mind:
Each tone, each word,
I hear again,
As once more
You walk away.

A single tear swells
And falls into the desert
Of my heart
Where sand sifts
Onto fallen ruins,
Hopes and dreams
Tossed aside.

At that same time, in November of 1991, Ruth learned that she had breast cancer—more specifically, inflammatory carcinoma—for which there was no cure. She underwent surgery for a double mastectomy and began a series of chemotherapy sessions, each one draining her more than the previous. I drove to Portland every other weekend throughout that winter and spring to visit with her.

My Three-Day-Weekend

Within the quiet eye of the tornado
Away from my routine,
I watched the debris of other lives
Swirl around me.

Ruth picked over wallpaper
Like tomatoes at the market;
In her head a vision that
No pattern conformed to fit.

Like high-wire aerialists
The squirrels performed
On a cable overhead.
Fat raindrops fed new plants;
While spring wind
Pruned away unneeded
Branches and leaves.

The rain sluiced the air and streets
With a spring housecleaning
Removing winter's clutter

Sisters—A Visit

Never long enough
Always crammed with words,
Ideas half-understood
Conversations unfinished
Topics unexplored

Saturday was just the same.
Five hours were not enough
To convey our feelings,
To explore each other's minds,
To rejuvenate our inner selves.

I left, wanting to remain,
Resenting the untimely intrusion
That tore me away
That ended the tarot
That left so much unsaid,

Until next time.

Ruth

As children, Ruth and I were cohorts in everything. We romped and played together, slept in the same bed, and got into trouble together. Yet, like all children, we grew in separate ways. As a teen I was quiet, reserved, and could be found with a book. Ruth was outspoken, rebellious, and liked popular music. We married within six months of each other, and though our paths diverged, we wrote many letters to each other.

By the time Deidre was ill, Ruth had married her third husband, Gary Fasching, and still lived in Portland, as did her three children and their families. Gradually, we reforged the broken strands of our childhood, learned to question rumors, and to laugh when something went just the way we anticipated.

Ruth was my sister, but also a friend. She listened to both Deidre and Bud and tried to explain me to them and them to me. We shared the problems of her alcoholism and my nerves. I started her in genealogy research, and she dragged me to yard sales. We read tarot cards for each other, and we gained clearer readings when we teamed than when we did solo readings. She played piano by ear; I read notes. She painted pictures that she saw in her head; I needed a photo and a detailed drawing on canvas before I could paint. She was my sounding board, and I was hers. We were the two halves that make a whole.

**

Part of learning to live is learning to accept sisters, not as bickering siblings but as adults, women with dreams, not unlike my own. Ruth and I, only two years apart in age, related well. Georgia, on the other hand, the little sister, the tag-a-long, was five years younger than I was. Looking back I find that we were never close. When I married at sixteen, she was only a child of eleven.

It was only as two college students that we became friends. She was a sophomore and I was a junior. We shared living quarters, and I drove us to college each day. She laughed with me when I'd hit the accelerator on my pale yellow Mustang and race the train headed toward North Powder. It was fun to see if we could reach the overpass before the train slid like a long snake beneath the highway.

When she set her wedding date, I made her dress, a long sleeveless sheath of white velvet. It was after the wedding that we moved apart. She moved to Ohio and nine months later gave birth to a baby girl. I still had no child, and she did not live close enough to share.

Over the years, she would tell me, "I'm not a writer." And, that was that. Still I wondered. It takes such little time to stay in touch. She went her way back and forth across the country when the air force moved her husband. She raised a family of four, two boys and two girls. Now, at home in Texas with a new partner, she remains distant and apart.

About this time, when I was creating the Schoenberger notebook to give our half-sister Margaret a sense of the family she had never known, Ruth wrote the following for me:

Who Is Carol?

She got married when she was sixteen years old and has one daughter who is grown and married. Her husband has worked on construction, and that has given them the chance to do quite a bit of traveling through the states. She would love to go to Europe.

She has spent many years of her life going to school; she has taught several years of school. She is sensitive with a broad view and a vivid imagination. She has been a perfectionist since she was a kid and is her own worst critic. She is a creative person and an artist. She is also a writer who has had several poems published. She would like to write a book.

She is a genealogist and loves research. She likes plants and animals; cats are her favorite animal. She has always been known to have her nose in a book. She spends hours on needlework and likes to make hand-sewn things. I can come up with an idea, and she can make it and sell it. Some of her things are for sale in shops. She likes antiques and collects carnival glass. She also has restored some old dolls and dressed them in fancy original costumes that she has made. She is a busy person and likes having things to do. She also likes her solitude.

Carol is my sister, and we are bonded close. There is something nice about being sisters that differs from being friends with anyone else. I think we have a mental compatibility, although we are as different as night and day. She is like my other half. We have fun together and can share our capabilities. We can talk for hours on end or be quiet together with nothing to share. We just mix and match and that is special. We seem to have a sixth-sense feeling together.

I can write Carol a letter, and she will write me one the same day, without knowing. I think about her, and she often calls me on the phone. I like her, and I certainly am glad that we are friends.

**

In 1992 Fossil School District hired me to teach grades seven through twelve, and Bud and I moved into a rental house in Fossil, finally leaving Dennis and Deidre alone in their own home. She and I had begun to relate as adults, not just as mother and daughter, and Dennis filled the vacancy left when Gerry died.

Mom

Were we the same age, we could be good friends.
As it is, there has never been an opportunity.

You raised me as a single mother would.
Even though you were married, he was never home.
You instilled in me values that I carry today:
Giving one's best effort, not giving up.

We are so much alike, you and I,
Too bad there were so many obstacles in the way.

When I was a child, you were always working.
As a teenager, our similarities brought us both grief.
Now that I'm grown, I understand you better,

But now our lives force us apart.

You've been my teacher, my guardian,
my friend,
But have always been restrained.

You had me later in life and had your
patterns set.
I won't analyze your parenting—you
did your best.
You were always distant; age, hobbies,
and what not,
But lady, I'm glad I've known you—
good times and bad.

Deidre L. Denham
October 20, 1992

In June and July of 1992, I responded to job offers appearing on teacher placement listings. I interviewed at Welches on the Mt. Hood highway, at North Marion High School north of Salem, at Monument, and then at Fossil in eastern Oregon. When I made the trips to Monument and Fossil, Ruth went with me. The trips tired her, but we both knew if she didn't go with me, she would not revisit these areas, as her husband Gary was a real homebody and did not like to travel. When we went to Monument, the peaches in Kimberly orchards had just begun to ripen. We took time to pick two boxes for her to share with her kids, and then spent the night with Margaret in Madras.

Ruth and I had tried several times to locate Margaret, our half-sister who had dropped out of sight after a divorce. I traced her from Union County to Pendleton and then to Echo and Arlington, but from there— nothing. By accident, after Ruth began genealogy, she learned that a cousin still wrote to Margaret's mother-in-law. Eventually, she learned that Margaret had married William Wise, a rancher near Arlington. She obtained Margaret's address, wrote to her, and learned that both were retired and living near Madras. From the visit in 1992, the three of us developed a friendship that somewhat bridged the missing years, and I promised to build Margaret a Schoenberger book to help her connect with Daddy and her missing roots.

When I returned from the interview at Fossil, a phone

call was waiting for me. The new superintendent of the Fossil district wanted me for the English opening at Wheeler High School. I began there in August. I had been out of the classroom for four years. In that time, Oregon had moved toward school reform. I had been involved with changes in the writing curriculum, but was unaware just how much more had changed.

I was one of three new teachers hired that year by a new superintendent. There was a new teacher in the science room, and Marian Hall was on staff for elementary music and counseling. Before the year was out, she and I became good friends.

Marian

A caressing wind of love,
Marian passes, felt but unseen,
Just on the edge of vision.
With open arms and hugs,
She reaches for life,
Accepting herself and others
While teaching students
And dreaming of France.

Marian and I enjoyed team-teaching, especially with writing. I could introduce and model a poetry-writing lesson, and Marian with her intuitive nature could influence the direction of the students' responses. Together, we evoked abilities that I don't believe I could have developed in students without her. Besides helping students, Marian helped me to understand what changes I needed to make as a teacher. Her training was more recent than mine and was more student-centered. We worked together, walked together, and shared ideas. We shared the emotional pain of our lives, and she was with me when Ruth passed away. Her intuitive understanding helped me begin to stretch and grow. She gave me a copy of *Women Who Run With Wolves,* a book that set my reading on the path of women's studies. I moved on to read *Goddesses in Every Woman* and *The Feminine Face of God.* I bought a copy of *Sisters of the Earth* and began reading Lynn V. Andrews's books describing her spiritual journey.

Ruth's cancer continued to take its toll, and with each treatment she became frailer. Gary took her to the hospital in December 1992, and then to a nursing home because she did not want to leave the memory of death in her home.

To Ruth, January 7, 1993

A letter, a poem? Who knows…
Communication, to be sure

Gary called last night,
When the lights were out
And snow drifted lazily under the
streetlight.

His voice was clear, unfettered with
dread,
As he told me that you were home.
The joy he felt vibrated across the miles,
To lift my spirits and let them soar.

The elation in his voice as he shared
the settling in, the preparation,
the finding of your long-lost ring.
He said he wanted to staple it to your
finger
But that you wouldn't let him.

He groused about the Home and its
"uncare."
I hear you had Stick-ups by the clutch
More than the room would hold
To freshen the air and deaden the stench
of neglect.

While he spoke, you were sitting
drinking coffee,
So he said. That you'd been settled in
for only ten minutes

Or so—didn't want to talk. But that was
okay.

He shared the egg-crate mattress, the
oxygen,
Hospice, Sandi and Ron sitting with
you...
And beneath it all, I heard a strong river
of relief.

You were home
His circle was again complete.
He stood ten feet tall over the phone
As he retold the doctor that he could
care for you
"Better than anyone else."

He can too. We both know that.

Love Is All There Is

The porcelain fragility
     Of your voice
     That echoed bell-like
     Across the miles
     Fell
     Last night
     As rice paper
     Onto a dry tatami mat.

Your words came…slow…
"I never thought I'd live dying…
I am so loved…
Remember, love is all there is."

     Silence…
     You breathed…
"I'm so tired now…"
     The thin blue line of life
     Attenuates:
     How much longer, dear Lord,
     Until it parts?

In early February, Ruth's son Ron phoned to tell me
she was gone.

You Had to Go

"Remember,
Love is all there is,"
You said when last we spoke.
What we didn't speak of
Was the ache,
The unshed tears,
The parting…

We knew, you and I,
That you would have to go
While I remained…
To remember.

Saturday's moon shone full…
Red as it rose above
Windswept barren hills…
Pale, luminous
With Venus beckoning in the west.

You rode with me then,
And yesterday…
Across the snow covered Blues,
Along the frozen rivers,
Where green-white icy water
Broke through.
At Ritter
Under a sunwashed sky
The bald eagle stood proud
Above his prey.

Amid the quiet
You met his bold stare. . .
And we went on
Beneath the rims,
The shadowing pines.

I shared your peace:
The jesses fell away
And you soared free.

This was a year of turmoil. Ruth's death on February 6, 1993, was followed by that of Bud's father, Frank F. Crandell, on February 11, and the suicide of Forrest Ludwig, one of my eighth-grade students, just before school closed in May. To round things out, Marian was not rehired—the board considered her position a one-year attempt at enrichment for elementary students and to keep at-risk high school students from dropping out.

The Man I Knew—My Father-in-Law

A large man,
So he seemed when I was thirteen,
With a thick shock of grey-white hair,
A suit of pastel blue or grey or green,
And a Bible tucked within his arm.

I saw him, too, in uniform
Smudged with grease or oil
From working on a car.

He had a ready smile and
Boisterous laughter;
He liked people,
Good times
Good food
Friends.

Later, he said the words
That wed me to his son.

He was grandfather to my children,
One he never saw.
The other he watched as she cut teeth,
Laughed, and cried.
Grandpa held her high when she was five,
Her blond head against his white.

Her yearly photos decorated
His Colorado home:
He watched her grow, but from afar.
She grew up
Graduated
Wed her chosen,

And he was not there to share.
He missed so much
That only comes once in every life.
I see a lonely man
Who chose a path that led away
From family and friends.
We missed him
As he filled his life
With others
Who were not us.

I'm sorry
We couldn't share our
Life, creating
Memories
To fill the empty days.

In March 1993, conflict over junior high students came to a head. These students were attending some of their classes in the high school where the high school teachers taught them. Parents approved of subject area experts, but did not want their children mixing in the halls with older students. Following a parent/staff meeting, seventh- and eighth-graders remained at the high school for their science class, but the math teacher and I spent the remainder of the year walking back and forth between the high school and the elementary building, two blocks away.

Shell Shocked

This morning
White rounded hills
Bleed into a grey-white sky,
Heavy like the soul within me,
Shuttered and crying.

What use to share, to plan?
To dream a dream?
The wall of anger
Like Berlin concrete
Divided.

Mostly silent we sat
Unheeded, unneeded,
Pinned beneath the barrage of
"We want! You will!"

This is not consensus.

The Last Good-bye

Golden light stroked a land
Green with new spring growth;
Sunflowers nodded gently
Under an east wind's caress;

The meadowlark atop the hill
Beckoned me onward
Along the sandy road
And step by careful step
Upward, ever upward.

I parted the blue-grey sage,
Inhaled the too-sweet scent
Of newly blossomed greasewood
And paused.

A riot of spring green
Lay spread before me,
A patchwork of color
Pieced together by birdsong,
Scent, and love.

You were there with eyes alight,
Flaxen hair slightly tousled by the breeze,
A wide grin of delight upon your face,
And no earthly bonds restrained you
As you spread your arms to fly.

I shut my eyes and you are here.
I'll miss your knowing smile,
The challenge in your question,
Your readiness to do things your way
Or to play…

Your stay was short
Before your star led onward
Beyond us,
To do what only you
Knew how to do,
Or go where only you
Knew you had to be.

During this stressful time, Bud chose to read my journals. Ten years earlier, I had written them for him, as I was unable to talk about the problems bothering me. He'd never read the journal that I tucked into his backpack. He told me, "I was afraid to know you that well." I did not think of my journals as incriminating, so kept them shelved with my books in the library. He began reading them without my knowledge and took entries out of context. When he accosted me about the material he said, "I've known about your affair since Pennsylvania, and I have a tape to prove it." He had said nothing for six years. Now, he did not want to hear anything from me. There was no room for explanation or discussion. Lightning struck, leaving desolation in its wake. There was no room for understanding.

"I don't think we even like each other anymore," I said. "We might as well split."

He agreed. "You will get your divorce—but only when I'm ready." Which wasn't then.

Riven Rock

The stone wall so carefully laid
to withstand wind, and rain, and hail
shows gaps where fell the blows.
Lonely rocks…
dislodged and fallen
lie atop the spring green moss.

Stress cracks
in grey heartstone
etched with orange-red lichen
tell of inner pain, concealed.

Still strong, this wall endures
shielded by brown needles
of a sheltering pine.

Blackened clouds roil the air,
electric streaks of light
crisscross and strike,
riving me apart.

Amid the sulfurous haze
the pine lies rent;
fragments of stone lie
tossed across the slope…
remnants…
lost hopes and dreams.
I must now decide:
Just endure, or live?

I had accepted renewal of my contract for a second year, and life went on. We slept in the same bed but never touched. Bud went out of his way not to irritate me when he was home. Still, I knew that I needed to prepare for an ending, but how did I start? I called legal aid for advice and almost panicked. Calling credit card companies to establish my own credit rating was worse. Doing these little chores forced me to acknowledge the separation—my first visible steps of growth.

**

As I read Lynn Andrew's books relating her spiritual journey as she studied the Native American traditions, I found one book that described her work with the her Lakota wise woman. This woman instructed Lynn to create a medicine shield, gave her the willow for a hoop and left her to discover her way. Reading between the lines in July of 1993, I began to gather materials and create my first shield. I began with the south shield, representative of my childhood and beginnings in eastern Oregon. I selected a creamy chamois skin— the dry desert—and laced it onto a green-willow hoop. I learned that one does not use a green-willow hoop without tightening the lacing several times, as the hoop shrinks. Using acrylic paints, I depicted a basalt-capped bluff dominating the right side, a juniper to the left, a wolf leaping from a full moon at the top, and both a wolf print and my handprint in the foreground. The bluff shows my deep-rooted love of the rim rocks of the John Day River country and for Black Butte that loomed over my home in Fossil. My wolf is the wild spirit, the child hidden and crying for release from within, and the moon represents a subtle yet dominating force in my life. The paw print is the wolf inside lying hidden beneath a civilized exterior, and my handprint is the unifying element—my will that dominates. I knew when I finished this shield that I would create another, but I did not know when.

My second year at Fossil, 1993–94, was busy but stressful. I spent the summer writing a plan for a talented and gifted program (TAG) and a writing workshop curriculum to use with my English classes. In August, the superintendent moved my classes from the library to a larger classroom, displacing the social science teacher, Mr. Knapp. This move caused mixed feelings among students and staff once classes resumed. Using the TAG plan that I had written, I spent part of my day in the elementary classrooms or with identified students providing enrichment activities. At the high school, I used a senior-project approach with upper-level students, trying to individualize for both interest and ability.

I encouraged all of my students to write for publication in the school paper. Because of student opinions in persuasive essays, some parents again became angry and upset because I would not censor topics that were important to the students, even though mothers thought that their students should not discuss topics such as safe sex and abortion.

This issue also led to problems with a board member who skirted school policy to discuss publication issues and guidelines with students instead of coming to me. Then I angered another mother because I expected her son to behave in class, and was chewed out over the phone by a father who thought I should excuse his son for missing deadlines. Before the dust of this settled, I was accused of having an affair with the superintendent because we spent too much time working together on curriculum, student scheduling, school-reform issues, and a plan for a block schedule and cooperative schooling with the neighboring school in Condon.

Even so, I wrote "Guardians," published in *In the Desert Sun*, "Winter Music," and others.

Guardians

The line we tread
       bounds the butte
       just north of town…
       an unseen fence
       beside barbed wire
       that bears "No Hunting"
       on an aged post.

When we have passed
       and dark has come,
       coyotes pace the northern rim
       beyond our path.

Toward the south
       where children sleep,
       vows are made…
       the guard is changed.

In 1993, I also completed my west shield, which represented emotions and death—the turmoil of adulthood. For the coolness of the Oregon coast, I laced grey pigskin onto a second willow hoop. I painted the ocean and beach with an offshore haystack rock beyond a rocky bluff. I feel a deep need—a pull of the ocean—especially during times of emotional turmoil. A mountain cat steps softly between the rock and bluff, half-seen behind two spruce trees. The Pacific Ocean is the tide in my blood and holds a dolphin—my subconscious, a messenger from the underworld. The cat shows a wildness, a need deep within. The tiny shells, flowers, and rocks represent my beachcombing, the colors I see, and the trees that sing in the wind—my love of Nature and her beauty.

Winter Music

Again I paced the trail
Between now and what will be,
Through an uncertain light,
Neither cloud, nor mist…but ghostly fog
That wrapped the butte
In warmth of winter wool.

Roadside grass and mustard tumbleweeds
Stood clear along the way
Their feathered fronds and spiky stems
Encased in velvet ice.
As if transported to a winter ball
The junipers stood tall
Clad in silvery brocade coats;
While sage with fluttering fans
And skirts of lace
Held court along the wall.

An eerie music from an ancient harp
Drifted on the air;
Unheard except by silent dancers,
It lodged within my soul.

In the spring of 1994, Mother stayed with us for two weeks. She had been living in the Willamette Valley and was stopped for erratic driving on the freeway. My niece Sandra rescued her and phoned us. She refused to keep Mom with her and wanted me to take charge. Bud met them in The Dalles and brought Mother to Fossil, as her home in Union was a wreck. The renters who had lived there left after trashing the house. Mother wanted to remain independent and manage her own affairs, but she could not go home until her house had been cleaned, repaired, and painted. Bud took time to make repairs and move her back to Union.

As spring moved into the hills, I felt the need to begin the third, or north shield, representing intellect and wisdom. Again, I selected grey pigskin for its sense of elusiveness, or mystery, as all is neither black nor white in my world. I knew that the shield would be bisected vertically by a stream, representing the importance of water in my world, and that the left, or west side, would represent western Oregon. I painted a foreground of green meadow receding into hills with trees backed by snowcapped mountains. Behind the mountains, six phases of the moon rise to meet the midday sun. The moon, the orbiting body that most influences my moods, also symbolizes death and rebirth. The sun is light that is necessary in my life and shows growth in knowledge or wisdom. When I began to lay the design for the right side, I was stymied. I was forced to put the project aside and did not return to it until the following winter.

North Shield

North with its white comes hard
Divided into halves. The west,
White mountains and green trees
Comes live.
East, the desert, set apart
By the river…waters of my life…
Lies dormant, unseen.

Do I paint alkali hills?
Do I walk sagebrush flats?
I wanted a tree; it doesn't fit.
North: maturity, wisdom,
All come hard.
Learning takes time;
Smart doesn't mean wise.
Slow down.
Wait.
Let the heart learn.
It will feel the rightness
When the spirit knows.

In March, the Fossil district offered me a contract for another year; however, beyond that was doubtful since they were cutting back expenses—which meant programs. Cutting the TAG program would shave $10,000 from my position, and would remove my incentive to remain with the district. Because I was one of the higher-salaried teachers and would be due for permanent status, nonrenewal of my contract would allow the district to hire a new teacher for less money.

Because of this uncertainty and the atmosphere in the town, I updated my placement file with Eastern Oregon State College in April of 1994, and again began reading job lists. In early May, I interviewed at Harper School, a small, rural district located on the Highway 20 west of Vale, Oregon. Jim Payne, the superintendent, had warned me that the region had few, if any trees. He was right. After leaving the mountains north of Unity, there were no more pines and few junipers. As far as the eye could see, sagebrush covered the land. That spring was also windy. With little to break its force, the wind swirled the dust into clouds that looked like fog. I wasn't sure about the Malheur County climate, but I did know that I was ready to leave Fossil. Within a week, I had accepted their offer, resigned from Wheeler High in Fossil, and by Memorial Day weekend, had rented a house.

Desert Decisions

Two years past I moved
East to Fossil and the desert.
Here, red-brown basalt caps the hills;
Grey sage clumps on dry grass slopes.

Noontime sunlight falls on fragrant
Pine needles and dry cones;
Fire-red poppies riot midst yellow iris that
Hug the warm grey wall.

Always when I walk my line
Black Butte is there,
A tower, a bulwark of strength,
Solid in its silence.

I climbed its talus slopes,
Paced the wandering trails,
Clambered up a narrow chimney,
Until I could stand

Upon the topmost point
With wind gusting in my face.
I looked beyond the bounds
Of daily space and time

To blue mountains, forests,
And river breaks that lay
Outside the valley
Where I live each day.

Now, an eastern desert calls.
It lacks juniper and basalt,
But sage grows there
In sandy soil.

The decision made:
A risk awaits.

As soon as I finished my school obligations in June, we began moving from Fossil to Harper. Again, I sorted things for storage. This time, my dome-top trunk containing childhood mementos, Gerry's baby record, our wedding book, my journals, and other keepsakes went to Union for storage. Bud's sister Carol and her husband Bill came with their pickup to help us. It took several trips, but eventually the Fossil residence was empty and I began to settle the new house into a home. Then it was time for a one-week Summer Institute, continued training in school reform, to be held in The Dalles.

Desert Notes

Pungent pine and fir give way,
No heady juniper stands guard,
Tall white mountain peaks retreat,
Exchanged for rugged, rock-capped buttes.
The pronghorn jounces thru low grey sage
While mule deer pause
To peer my way.
A mourning dove, unseen,
"Uh, uh, oos" upon the wind,
And crickets chirr beneath the step.
Brown water chuckles within a ditch,
And green frogs pipe along its bank.
Caressed by sound,
My heart finds peace
As the full midsummer moon sails
Above the ridge
To cast strange shadows on the sand.
An ancient, half-felt magic stirs
And calls me out.

As school in Harper began in the fall, Bud left to work in Arlington. We had finally traded the large fifth-wheel trailer for a smaller one that he was comfortable pulling with his pickup. He lived in this for most of that winter. Again, I was starting over in a new classroom with new students, trying to meet their needs and plan lessons to help them achieve needed skills. In evenings, I worked on the genealogy material Ruth had left behind, putting it together in notebook form for her husband and her three children. She had asked me to undertake this task when she knew that she would not live to finish it. I also continued to write poems along with my students in creative writing.

The Tiger Behind My Back

My feet trod upon a dusty road,
Yet I wandered through a mist
Where time did not exist,
And diversion was a tiger,
My worries come to life.

It paced me on the right
Just beyond my sight,
Yet hemmed me in
Constraining every step,
Hampering each and every move.

To shut out that regular
In and out of breath,
To banish the hunter on my trail
Became a must.

For me to move ahead.
It became necessary to let go,
To step off into the fog that hid my way,
To leave behind my *shoulds* and *shouldn'ts*,
To see beyond the here and now.

Some dreams are evanescent, half-remembered upon awaking. Others hold portent of things to come, if I listen closely. One such dream woke me during the still hours of the night. I still felt warm arms holding me close, but could not tell where I was standing, or when it happened.

Dreams

Dreams of other times, other places
Gateways to the beyond
A room where I've never been
Someone I know, but I've never seen
A yearning for something
Pulled toward someone
Unresolved feelings
Warnings
A hug from afar
Loose ends in my life
Frayed by time
Gathered, knotted
Rebound as I wake.

Notes from the Desert

Beside the Malheur
Where now I make a home,
Harper roads are rock and sand.
No streetlights glow on corners;
No stoplight turns red or green;
Time moves to a slower, saner beat
With deer and stripey skunks the only vagrants.

Along the roads
Fall cottonwoods and elms
Cast tired leaves in drifts to turn
And twist into the wind,
To flutter, to fall, to nestle,
A crackly quilt upon the ground,
To warm the earth
Where next year's roses sleep.

On Halloween
When unseen worlds are said to touch,
The air was chill.
No moon shone forth to light the way
For small ghosts and painted creatures
Trekking to my door.
The year has turned
Bringing gold to edge the brown
Of sand and sage.
Cattle are pastured,
Hay sheds are filled,
All crops are in,
And geese are on the wing.
Coyotes yip and call
Beneath surrounding chalk-white buttes;

A lone hawk soars aloft
Gliding 'cross the land,
Then stoops and dives
To seize his dinner on the run.

Quiet settles here.
Where no Amtrak rockets past,
I hear the quiet call of quail
Along the ditch;
I hear a lone leaf rustle
In its fall onto the grass.
Wind whispers and complains
Bending branches, tumbling weeds,
Prying into cracks around the door.

Days dwindle in length
As winter approaches,
Creeping into the valley on soft-padded paws.
Snow soon will arrive
To cling to red mittens
And powder the land,
To soften the blemishes,
To erase scars made by man,
To invigorate roots, swell seeds,
And mark time until spring.

Winter and Christmas were approaching when I returned to my shield project six months after the move from Fossil. As I looked at the half-painted canvas, I knew deep inside that the Malheur desert and chalk hills to the north of Harper were meant for the blank side of the picture. They balanced the green, the two physical worlds in which I have lived my life. The distinct geographic differences resemble the split in my life—the mental and emotional agony, the divisiveness that has molded my character. Between the two sections, I painted a winding river—the John Day, the Mississippi—all the waters in my world. I created a fallen snag, my broken relationship, from a piece of juniper broken from a fallen tree on the top of Black Butte. I added a rail fence of small twigs to keep dangers outside, but also a reminder to me that like a rock wall, the fence can become a prison for the inner self. The creatures of the desert—coyote, owl, and raven—each have a place in this picture. These are for me harbingers of change.

Following my reading of *Oak, Ash & Thorn*, a book about Celtic spirituality in May 1995, I took the piece of golden buckskin that Marian had brought me from Ashland, Oregon, and began on the east shield that represents spiritual growth. The golden color of the leather reflects the light of knowing. A large tree with spreading branches, the world tree of Norse mythology, arises from the midst of Stonehenge. A silver stair spirals the tree, rising into the upper branches. It is reached by a rocky path winding up from the lower edge of the picture. This represents the pattern of my life, a gyre. I climb the stair high into the branches, seeking knowledge or descend the rocky path to seek within myself and to accept that which is hidden. Stonehenge represents my ties to the unknown past of the Celts and Britons.

**

Dennis took a job with Oregon Fish and Wildlife in John Day, and in the spring of 1995, moved Deidre to a house on the Holladay Ranch located between John Day and Prairie City. Bud began to get the Salem house ready to sell. By June, the remodeling was complete and the house listed with a realtor who sold it within the month. I had waited two years for Bud to indicate a move, but he was still hanging on. My sense of loyalty and fair play made it hard for me to push him. Yet, with the house sold and money in the bank, I told him that I wanted to file for divorce.

After I told Deidre and Dennis that we were divorcing, they told me that this was not a surprise. Deidre said she had expected it since she was five—remaining as a family did not provide her with stability and security. Instead, she was given uncertainty and the knowledge that all was not well in her world.

That winter she wrote the following poem. It was the way she believed that her father saw me—as a possession, not a partner.

China Doll

China doll
don't fall off your shelf
don't move a muscle
don't change from that picture-perfect pose

China doll
you're breakable
don't put yourself to that test
I'll take care of you

China doll
stay put
don't dirty your dress
don't muss your pretty hair

China doll
let someone else live your life
be a possession
be a trophy

China doll
don't ever say—
I won't stay on my shelf
I will not break

Deidre L. Denham

I thought we could do it ourselves without lawyers, and I even obtained the needed papers, but that is not how it worked. Bud came home for the summer but went to Fossil (taking the paperwork with him) for deer and elk hunting in late September and October. Finally, I phoned to tell him I wanted him to return so that we could get the legal process started. The next thing I knew, he had seen a lawyer in Fossil. Then when I tried to retain one in Vale, I found that Bud had already retained him and filed for divorce.

After Bud returned to Harper, we made a trip to Union so that I could get the family heirlooms and personal items that remained there in storage. "We are missing a trunk," I told him. "The dome-top one is gone." We tore the place apart, but it wasn't there. The chain and lock securing the storage shed had been cut with bolt cutters, a broken flashlight lay kicked aside on the floor. The antique lamp no longer stood beside a stack of boxes, and now, my trunk was missing.

I was devastated. I had adjusted to giving up the antiques and jewelry that Bud insisted were his, but losing the trunk was the last straw. My journals were lost; Gerry's baby mementos were gone; the chenille dog and stuffed skunk from my childhood—all gone. Gone too were antique dolls, a paisley throw, Ron's baby book, and all the varied items filling the trunk. Anger filled me—the things that meant the most to me had no resale value. Why would they be taken? This cut me loose from my past, and no ties remained.

I was not upset that Bud had filed before I could; however, he was going to fight. In Fossil he said, "I'll give you the divorce, but I want all of the antiques and the jewelry. You'll be lucky to keep the clothes on your back." He did everything possible to drag out the process. Over the next year, I conceded the antiques, the jewelry that he had given me for anniversaries and Christmases, and all of the property, including the coastal piece for which I had paid. I did this to prevent splitting my retirement fund with him. Finally, on May 26, 1996, he signed. Our lawyers submitted the papers to the court, and the judge signed in June. Thirty days later, we were single again. Thirty-seven years severed by three signatures.

My Evening Walk

Tonight I walked a rain-washed world
Though grey-blue clouds and thunder ruled the sky.
I jogged my way beside the green-fringed ditch
Where water chuckled on its way.
New green duckweed nestled 'neath
Cattail spikes now sporting heads of brown
Beside bright yellow sunflowers.
In the narrow path I walked lay clear-cut tracks
Where two does had crossed into the field.
And as I walked, I gleaned tiny bits of stone;
The first was red, another gold; a third
Held crystal at its heart, each a treasure
Offered by nature for my art.
Down Amick Road I passed
While wind fingers tangled in my hair.
The *tck-tck-tck* of rainbirds
Played counterpoint
To the clanking of a lead sheep's bell.
Then she came to me, the hawk,
Screeing in the wind while soaring o'er my head.
She led me onward, ever-circling
To settle on a perch beside her mate.
Together they lifted in aerial ballet
Circling, soaring, dipping with the wind
Always, just above my head.
And to my joy, there then were four
Calling to each other, lifting, swirling, settling.
With a lump in my throat and tears
I watched them in their freedom;
Then turned and traced my steps
While thunder rumbled and grey clouds

Rained upon my face.
I walked with raindrops on my lashes
And watched the mists obscure the hills.
At the last, the sun with promise
Cast a golden ladder through a breach
Between the clouds.
I saw them then, two does,
Pale in autumn dress.
With ears held high, they watched me come,
Then turned and bounced away
While I, alone, continued.

Chapter 13: Awakening

Desert Diamonds

Days grow shorter and nights colder
As the season turns. At midnight
I stand beneath a blue velvet sky that wears
A scatter of diamonds across her breast.
Coyotes in full chorus greet the full moon
As she glides beneath the Milky Way.
Her silvery light illumines my world
Creating shades that lean drunkenly
Across my path. I savor the solitude,
The crisp bell-like quiet that settles
Onto the valley like the soft sweatshirt
I pull close against the cold.

Morning now risen in colors of flame and rose,
Streaking over the clouds and sage hills
That bound the land, to wake the lone owl
Who cries his welcome to the dawn
As I walk the path to school.
Of moments such as these
My days are formed.
Laughter lights my days;
A newfound peace I hold within.

With joy, I greet each dawning:
With words and music, I pace the day
While students find themselves and
Their place within the shifting pattern
That is Life.
I guide and push and sometimes hug,

Learning comes hard;
Risking creates uncertainty;
Growth is difficult, yet we persist,
Stretch to reach the dreams we've dreamed,
To walk the pathways set by Fate.

The desert I embraced
Now holds my heart in thrall, and
Like the spreading oak
I've set my roots, my anchor
Against the winds of change that sweep
Across my life.

I can't say all of the years spent with Bud were bad. Being married to a man who goes a lot did give me a chance to travel and see new places and people. Had I made other choices, I would not have satisfied my sense of adventure with trips to British Columbia years ago, traveled most of the states, nor spent a Thanksgiving in Pennsylvania and a winter in Augusta, Georgia. I would not have lived in the Upper Peninsula, seen the Great Lakes, flown to Hartford, Connecticut, or visited New England. These trips took me through areas of my genealogy research, letting me see where ancestors had lived, and giving me chances to visit cemeteries, museums, and libraries. I gained a great deal. My biggest regret is to realize how life could have been fuller and more complete had the marriage relationship been different. We grew in separate ways and somewhere over the years lost the connections and the ability to communicate except in superficialities.

Every person met on life's path can be a teacher, if the traveler is open to the opportunity. I did learn while with Bud. Over time, I became less talkative and outgoing as I let him dominate center stage. I am quick to judge by appearances but have become more open-minded, yet I am wary of being hurt or used. When I believe in something, I can become stubborn or rigid, yet this weakness helps me persist with a task. I learned to be competent in my profession even though I felt unsure at home. I became efficient and organized, developing an inner strength that helped me accomplish my goals. This strength became a weakness if I took on more activities than I could handle. I need approval, and want to be liked; thus, I let others, including Bud, take advantage of me. Because I care and am intuitive, I dislike causing pain to someone else. This makes me reluctant to discipline children. Thus, I become too lenient. My ability to care led me to do too much for others and not enough for myself. I trust people too far because I want to see the good in everyone. Because he idealized me and put me on a shelf instead of walking beside me, I learned that love is letting go. He taught me that possessions cannot buy undying love, and when he took them away, I found that my writing and my art were my real treasures. Most of all, I learned that I was alone and could ultimately depend only on myself.

I am who I am now because of the choices that I've made. Had I done differently, who knows what path I would have taken. As it is, I have an education that I have never regretted, a daughter who I am proud to claim, a few continuing friends, poems that I have written, and talents that I use.

Memory Trails: My Sense of Self

From the dry southeast Oregon desert, I recall
Water: green waves careening toward a rocky beach,
      rushing, roaring, breaking into spray;
      white horsetails of foam streaking

Water: aqua tinted, not spawned in the Pacific,
      unique to the Gulf of Mexico
      where white sand holds grey-green sea grass
      swaying 'neath a late March breeze;

Water: rushing, cascading, tumbling down
      across brown moss-covered rocks
      o'er draped by green maples and low-hanging
vines;

Water: raindrops
      reflecting
      hanging, falling
      from the spring green leaf
      outside the room at Lewis and Clark;

Writing: Lewis and Clark with Kim Stafford,
      sharing ideas, making new friends,
      finding new facets of myself;
      I turn and light reveals
      the artist playing with color and shape,
      the crafter twining grapevines to thread
      with silver cord and crystals,
      the writer seeking precise words,
      the editor finding too many mistakes,
      the teacher guiding young writers at work,
      the mother snuggling a child or a kitten;

I turn again, moving from interest to interest,
    never a master of any
    yet learning, enjoying, growing
    into a sense of myself.

As I filled the evening hours after I was alone, I returned to my needlepoint tapestry and to my writing. I had created a book for Margaret—my attempt to share Dad and her unknown family with her. Yet, I had no copy for myself. I went through my material one more time, revised what I had written, and made books for both Deidre and myself. These copies included reminiscences, poetry, factual data, and photos—whatever I had gathered that would help create real people from sterile dates and events.

The Man in Blue Denim

I first met Pat Briley in May of 1994, when I moved to Harper, Oregon. Sitting in a recliner on his screened front porch, he called, "Come on in!" and with cigarette in hand, gestured a welcome. He was a man in his sixties who resembled my father. Pat stood a stocky five feet, ten inches, and had black greying hair worn swept up in front like Elvis. His blue eyes twinkled with humor or flashed like bits of cold steel in a tanned face that never lost its color. Scratches and scars from close encounters with wood or metal marked strong hands that were always warm and gentle, whether he was holding reins or scratching itchy mule ears. I see him most clearly sitting with a cigarette in his right hand, thumb braced against his teeth, and eyes focused somewhere in distant thought.

He was most comfortable in blue denim shirts that must have two pockets, one for his glasses, and one for his cigarettes and scribe. His blue Wrangler jeans were often faded and so worn that I had applied patches to the knees or to the butt because he sat on a battery while working on his pickup and the acid ate holes in the fabric. He told me he hated to change clothes: "It takes an extra half hour just to switch things from my pockets."

He walked with discomfort and a pronounced limp, as his left knee was worn out from injuries and five surgeries. Still, he persisted in disking the pasture or riding his old grey mule. He was a proud man who hated to ask for help. "I'm macho!" he told me with a grin as I fetched him a cup of coffee or moved a block of wood close for him to sit upon.

Pat was defined by his sense of family. He was the youngest of four brothers and a sister who grew up in a migrant family during the Depression. "I was the littlest," he says, "and if I got whupped, that kid'd have to work his way through all my brothers before it ended. We were like a fist. We stuck together. From little on, all I wanted was a family of my own."

"My wife will never have to work," he'd insisted when he married Betty at age seventeen—and even though he often worked two jobs, for forty-five years, until her death in 1995, she maintained their home. At the same time, he expected a woman to be her best. "Look in the mirror," he'd say, "and tell yourself you are the best there is! No woman should ever have to put up with a man just to have a roof over her head." Then, smelling of English Leather, cigarettes, and sometimes of cutting oil from his machining work, he'd hug me and say, "You're a keeper." With a daily dose of that philosophy, Pat taught me how to be myself.

I Have Loved

I have loved …
Crisp mornings when white frost clings
Turning golden grasses into crystal; and
Skies o'ercast with clouds like grey lint
Warm from the dryer;
The sunrise above the southeast hills—
First a flush of rose, then a narrow stripe of
Crimson flaring into orange; and
Sunsets, splashes of golden fire in clouds to the west;
The snowcapped peaks stretching upward
Above the skyline or rounded hills; and
Pine forests, green and pungent under
A late August sun; and too,
I have loved the sagebrush desert
Home to fox and hen,
That places a healing balm upon my troubled soul;
And the sage, green with new spring rain
Or yellow with fall pollen that floats free upon
The evening wind;
The piercing call of the lone hawk
Winging high above me; the stillness of
A bald eagle perched on a whitened branch
Above the river;
The velvet of a cat's fur beneath my fingers,
Warm and sensual to my touch;
The acrid smell of old manure
Fresh-spread on new-turned garden soil;
The fragrance of still green mums,
Clumps against the leaves and rocks
That form the borders of my yard.
And I have loved

The smell of clothes fresh from the wash;
Crisp brown leaves beneath my feet;
A road to walk that takes me away from cares and daily chores;
The smell of fresh-baked pizza after a day of shopping;
The crunch of a crisp apple that fills my mouth with tartness;
A pomegranate, red and bursting with tiny seeds of sourness;
The bite of cinnamon on my tongue as I devour
A roll hot from the oven;
The bell-like notes dropping from a harp that plays
Counterpoint to the ebb and flow of ocean surf; the
Ocean pounding against black and weathered rocks, beating
Within my veins to set a saner pace for me to walk;
The cutting edge of windblown sand refining the flesh
But also the spirit;
The cozy warmth of a wool rug under my bare feet;
The enfolding heat from a wood fire that
Chases winter from my bones.
And I love
The friends I've never had till now,
Whose open arms supported when I had need;
The caring and concern that strengthened my resolve;
The gentleness of touch that gave without demand;
The letting go that told me I could fly;
The strength that brought me back
To nestle within warm arms:
These, the threads that form my life,
Create the patterns wherein I walk.

Winter

Winter lies cold
Upon the desert, a world
Of frost-whitened sage,
Ice-rimmed rivers, and
Crisp arrows of geese in flight,
Black vees against
The stonewashed sky.
In mid-December, she
Romps and blusters
Scattering the last lone leaves
Across yards; tumbling
Sun-dried weeds into piles
Along the garden fence.
Her mornings creep slowly
Above the southern hills
Brushing sunset colors
Onto the cloudy canvas
Of a waning night, while
High above a crescent moon
Gathers starlight within her arms.
Winter is filled with quiet,
A world of snowfall,
Sunshine, fog, or star shine;
She is the wood fire
Crackling in the stove;
She is the looking inward;
She is an ending;
She is a beginning.

Rainy Days

I've learned what rainy days are for
Besides washing the desert
Dust out of the air.
Rainy days are for:
Curling up with a book;
Dicing chicken and veggies
To make soup that teases senses;
Baking golden cornbread
To eat with strawberry jam:
Snuggling into a sweatshirt;
Toasting next to a wood fire;
Listening to old favorites
On an eight-track tape.
Rainy days are for sharing
    Quiet touches
    Gentle looks...
Arms close around me.

Fragility

I watched the sun rise
Through a mist of pearly rose,
A thin wash of paint smeared across the air.

Against the fence beaded with crystal drops of dew,
Purple iris and pale
Yellow roses
Caught the morning light.
A single languid rose revealed its heart,
The largest, outer petal falling
Away like the train trailing
On a lady's gown.

Shadows fell
As fluted edges caught the sun
Rippling like wavelets
On a garden pool.

The moment passed, and
Soon the sun,
A ship's flare,
Hung burning
Above the hills.

Pat brought stability into my life. He gave me friendship, companionship, and love. His openness broke through my barriers and helped me to find the me I had hidden away. Although we never married, he asked me to share his life and his home, and in the giving, granted me freedom to find my way.

I remained in the classroom at Harper School for two more years, but each day I found it more difficult to leave my life outside of school to spend time teaching students. My days centered on Pat and his projects. I learned about the process of machining as he built parts on his lathe or milling machine; I fed the mules, Sparky and Benj; and I began to turn a drab yard into one vibrant with flowers. Pat shared his ideas, and I drew the sketches for his parts. He read the drafts of my writing and offered insights and ideas, or pointed out spots that did not work. I then moved to the computer for revision and more writing.

While I remained in the classroom, Pat pushed me to build for retirement. With his encouragement, I invested in an annuity with the bank and another with a growth fund, added to my IRA, and built a savings account— all of which enabled us to purchase eighty acres of rangeland. This new feeling of financial security made it possible for me to retire from the classroom in June of 1998.

My final shield (the inner self) came together the summer of 1996 while my friend Marion spent a week with Pat and me. For leather, I selected black and emerald green remnants left from two masks that I'd created for Deidre and Dennis. This again reflected the division in my life. A grey leather mask to cover the true self—flanked by hawk wings that show the inner person's need to fly—dominated the center of the shield. Below the mask draped a necklet of porcupine quills fastened to a strip of red leather—my sharp, pointy protection. Silver earrings hanging from each side of the mask, and a grey rabbit-skin headdress reflected the importance that I place on the act of sharing. Marian gifted me with both items. Besides, the silver held a soft, reflective beauty, and the rabbit fur with its grey softness was velvety to the touch. At the bottom, below the quills were two hands clasped in friendship, sharing, companionship, and love. Each wrist bears a bracelet, one of turquoise and silver, the other of beads and silver charms. This joining of hands bridged the separateness in my life. I have learned that although I was alone, someone stood beside me—perhaps with love, perhaps with caring and trust. I now understood that each one of us must walk a path alone, but it does not have to be lonely. I am not an island, but a part of the *all*. My years of personal turmoil have been necessary for inner growth.

Wheel of Time

Today, I wander through halls
Half lit with memory
While echoes of laughter, and
Peals of joy resound
Against quiet tears
That slide in silence down my face.

I peer through time
To other days;
The babe is gone—
The woman flown.
Cords are now stretched thin—
Tenuous links connecting
Youth and age.

Life forces growth,
From seed, to plant, to flower,
And yet, to seed again.
I move upon life's wheel
Crawling, walking,
Running, limping, halting,
Retracing steps and lessons
As I strive,
As I seek
For understanding,
For the heart;
For why I am here.

Chapter 14: Living

Weather Change

An Arctic front moves on
Jostled aside by winds
From southern climes,
Gone, the sun that lifts the heart
And gives a lighter step;
Gone, the frost that coats the grass
Erasing definition.

Late Fall

Yellow leaves fall
From darkening limbs,
Drift across the sun-warmed
Shadows of a shingled roof,
Leaving
A single coin of gold
Caught in fractured wood.

The season passes
In a drift of floating milkweed,
A moment half-seen,
A thought uncompleted.

September Shower

Heads, both dark and blond
Bend over lined paper
As fingers tightly wrapped
Around the pencil
Form words to convey
Answers, black upon white,

A sudden spatter, raindrops
Upon dusty asphalt, and heads
Lift: "We left the car window open!"
"No, I closed it."…a mutter that
Dies away.

Thunder overhead rumbles;
Sunlight dims;
Dusty leaves stir and settle
Under a breeze's errant touch,
Moisture shines wetly
On the metal shop roof,
A telltale sign,
The overflow
Of a dark cloud's passing.

The Measure of a Year

The fall equinoctial moon,
Last seen in a predawn sky,
Waned to the merest sliver
And passed, marking
The close of another season
In my life.

I measure the time
By completion of the fifth medicine shield
That ends one cycle of inner growth;
By the finished tapestry
Begun some six years past;
By the petunias and marigolds
That still flaunt their purple
And orange around the yard; and
By the number of jars filled
With garden's bounty from the summer.

I see the year's passage
In the red of sumac and Virginia creeper,
In the yellow leaves of cottonwood and elm,
And in the grey of the doe's fall coat.

I measure the year
In the contentment and joy
Of planning and sharing.
I measure my days with happiness
And peace.

First Snowfall

Out of the grey dark sky
The first icy bits of crystal drifted
One by one
Bringing the season's first snow.

The roof,
Lean branches of elm,
The power cable
(a twisted braid of black and white,)
All wear a dusting of powdered sugar.

Flakes like fine snowy owl feathers
Continue to fall,
A lacy curtain
Filtering my view of the day.

Under the Desert Sky

Deep in remote reaches
Of Oregon's high desert
East of the Cascades,
Solitude is for sale.

A land of shimmering heat
And biting cold lies
Nearly a mile high…
Desolate, remote, unforgiving…

Where a tapestry of blue-green sage
Drapes across mountain and rim rock
Studded with emerald strands of juniper
Shaded softly by pastel sunsets.

In this wilderness of uncommon beauty
Outposts survive
Tethered by ribbons
Of asphalt without character.

Writing has been a major part of my life for almost thirty years. As a graduate student, I added fiction and poetry to my writing skills. As a teacher, I wrote course outlines and lesson plans. As a professional, I wrote plans to administer the TAG and English as Second Language programs. As the resident English "expert," I assisted with the revision and editing of the district policy manual, and as site council chairperson, I led in the development and writing of a portfolio plan, a technology plan, and a district improvement plan. I continued to write occasional poetry, added to my "in process" novel, and began work on *Merry-Go-Round*.

Night Rider

(for Lonie)

A thin sliver of moon
With the sheen of old silver
Drifted, half-seen behind
Cloud steeds galloping
Across sagebrush hills,
And slipped silently
Into the infinity
Of another time and place.

Following my retirement from Harper School in June of 1998, I remained with the district as the school improvement coordinator. This position included management of the library, assessment and analysis, coordinating surveys, writing a school profile, and myriad duties that teachers have no time to do. Yet this required only a small portion of my time. More important to me were the tasks centered on my writing, our yard, and the animals.

After the Rain

Gone, the desert heat of summer days
That sucks the moisture from all that lives;
Gone, the flowers of purple and gold
That draw the murmuring honeybees;
Gone, with the first fall rain.

In their place, the golden flame of cottonwoods,
Leaves that rustle in a colder breeze,
And a skitter of sunlight caught dancing
On the rain-washed blue reflection
In the greenish brown water of the river
Edged with a red and orange tapestry
Of wild rose and willow.

After the rain, the air is clear,
The juniper and sage clean-leafed
And redolent of resin.
Spikes of fawn-colored wheatgrass stand tall
Against grey-green sage contouring the wash
That shelters the fall-grey doe with her fawn,
And hides the tawny badger's den.

At night, the coyotes own the field.
Their yips against the quiet of the stars
Echo their pleasure of the hunt
While from the tall tree out back
The resident owl shrieks his presence
As he launches on silent wings…
After the first fall rain.

Chapter 15: Quality Time

Into the Desert

When I came to the desert region south of Unity, Oregon, I realized my new boss, Jim, had been right when he said that there weren't any trees here. All I could see was sagebrush.

The tall pines of the Blue Mountains had ceded space to junipers that had been defeated in the arid desert. Grey sage stretched for miles across hills and flatland, unrelieved except for hayfields irrigated by deep wells. Wind blew, moving topsoil in a thick cloud of dust across the highway from the newly prepared ground on one side of the road to a sage flat on the other. It blew all that spring, shifting soil, rolling tumbleweeds, and driving dust through every open crevice in the houses and barns that sparsely populated the region. Not the best of beginnings, but I chose to stay and called this region home for sixteen years.

May was a hot and windy month that year, and it led to a furnace-like summer that burned the hills a desolate brown. This was so unlike the time four years later, 2000, with lilacs perfuming the yard until a sneaky frost slipped in and blackened tender foliage. The spring of 2000 did bring rain and sun and they conspired to produce abundant grass on both low pastures and rangeland.

In April of 2004, we moved two horses and four mules onto our eighty acres of sagebrush range that lay a twenty-minute drive into the hills, across the irrigation canal, and through three gates. Each trip and the years that passed offered something of interest.

Laddie, our cow dog, watched for cows and calves. I spotted a red-tailed hawk riding a thermal above the ridge, or if I was lucky, I would see a golden eagle with sunlight glancing off his wings. As Pat and I topped the first hill, we often spotted a single antelope; she had been here before with a baby, and now she had another lying hidden amid the sage and bunch grass.

Along the winding dirt road, wild flowers flourished following spring rains. Purple lupine nestled amid grey sage in the more fertile soil. Pink and white low-growing flowers added sparks of color between green clumps of crested wheatgrass. Yellow-headed parsley clustered next to red-brown rocks and fuzzy pink onion heads intermingled with tarweed and cheat grass.

On the ridge just outside our gate, I found a new flower—a cluster of three blooms with waxy, pinkish white petals. It sprung right out of the barren, rocky soil with no obvious stem or leaves. My book named it as bitterroot, a plant favored by the Indians. The ridge sported grey sage, greasewood with its tender green shoots, and hopsage blooming in clumps of greenish yellow or reddish orange.

Jock, the red mule colt, would bray a welcome as we dropped off the ridge. Dancer, the grey part-Arabian gelding who tossed his head and hoisted his tail like a banner, followed him. Next came the mules, Patches and Benj. Sparky, the black mule, aged thirty-one, brought up the rear with Star, a Quarter horse mare, watching out for him.

Thus began two hours of what we called "quality time." Each animal knew its place. Jock went willingly to the round corral, Dancer walked to his designated post, Star waited patiently for her halter, and the mules found their feed pans. Patches became impatient, and as I brought in the grain bucket, he picked up his pan with his teeth and dropped it at my feet.

While they ate, we sat on the tailgate of the pickup, listening to the quiet. In that stillness, we heard the contented crunch of teeth chewing oats and corn. I heard the rooster pheasant chuckle to a hen in the wetland cattails below the canal. Two ducks startled from the water, quacking their indignation at some small disturbance. On a nearby fencepost a yellow-breasted meadowlark auditioned his love song, and a mourning dove sent a lonesome call from a distant elm tree.

Before releasing the animals, I had made the rounds with brush and comb, followed by a rubdown with an insecticide that helped them against the flies. Then they demanded their one-on-one time. Jock grabbed for my straw hat and laid his head on my shoulder as I rubbed the insides of his ears. Sparky demanded his cigarette and a belly rub. Dancer asked for a face and chin scratch, while Star wanted hands all over her. Benj wanted an ear rub and then turned to get his tail scratched, while Patches settled for a face rub and a pat on the neck. After a mule hug, it was time to leave.

Not all trips had ended this pleasantly. One week, the sun was shining as we moved metal panels up to the square pen. Suddenly, while we were securing the panels, a cold wind slammed against the corral and swirled the dust into a miniature tornado. When my eyes cleared, one glance to the west showed rain, white like snow, striding across the hills. We dove for the pickup just as the towering black cloud let loose over our heads. Quarter-sized raindrops pelted the windshield for a few minutes and then moved on across the valley. The sudden shower didn't turn dust to gluey mud, but it freshened the air. I smelled the pungent sage and the mushroomy odor of damp dirt as we left the corral and headed back up the ridge.

No sirens here, no noisy crowds, only the distant rumble of thunder, a mule's bray, and a horse's welcoming whinny. Daily frustrations and cares fell away, absorbed into the ever-present stillness of the desert, the solitude of a hermit's sanctuary. These wonderful years created vivid memories in my heart and mind. One of these is the story of Jock, our "bargain colt".

"There they are," I said, pointing to a pasture east of the highway. Both colts came to the fence as we pulled onto the shoulder and stopped the pickup just north of Brogan.

The flashy sorrel-and-white paint held back as I extended my hand for her to sniff. The second, a bit smaller and reddish in color, shoved in for a nose rub. A thick bandage obscured his off front leg from knee to hock; sutures closed long cuts on both upper legs and across his chest; and something had formed a lemon-sized lump on his neck. We learned that he had followed a jack, a male donkey, through a barbed-wire fence. As a yearling, the colt's strength and speed had intimidated his owner, a businessman in a rural community. He wanted to sell the colt, but we didn't need another animal, especially for $500. We could already see dollar signs for the vet. After thirty minutes of dickering, the owner said, "I really want you to have him. People have told me that your mules are the best cared for in the whole county. Will you give me $250?" Now that was a bargain price for a mule colt when a stud fee was $300. We hauled him home.

What I did not know about mules would fill several volumes, but I was willing to learn. After all, a yearling is only a baby, right? Right! But this baby had been hurt. With his good leg, he would strike like a snake if I even looked at his wound. How could I doctor him if he wouldn't stand still? With the medicines in squirt bottles, we found we could shoot a stream onto his leg, maybe applying enough to help. By accident, I discovered that a gloved finger rubbing inside his ear could distract him from his leg.

But proud flesh covered the wound, creating an ugly knot on his lower pastern. Back to the vet we went. Surgical removal of the tissue required a tranquilizer. Not hard for the vet trained to give shots, especially when the animal is in stocks, a narrow stall-like frame made of welded four-inch pipe, right? Think again. With the first jab of the needle, Jock jerked away. At the next attempt, he reared up and over the stocks and landed in the chair where I had been seated just seconds before and went down. The vet completed the injection then. "That's the only animal ever to get over those stocks," he said wiping sweat from his forehead. "He can jump like a damn jackrabbit. Let's get him out on the grass before he goes down." An hour later, following open-air surgery, Jock was back on his feet, into the trailer, and headed home to his corral.

In recovery, he demanded more than baled alfalfa and oats. He insisted on green grass, which meant we grazed him on a halter rope. That required a stronger arm than I had, so he did not always get grass when he wanted it.

His brays began at daylight and continued whenever he saw a person. Oh yes—he learned that he could lie down and roll under the lowest rail on a five-foot metal panel. That meant he now had the haystack and grass within nose reach, and he was out minus a halter. After this escapade and a headlong runaway, we took him to the mountains for the summer. He ran with the ranch horses, but if you called his name or whistled, he would bray an answer, betraying the herd's location. During this time, he learned to steal gloves or a wallet from a hip pocket and to eat hotcakes from a tin plate on the cook-shack table.

Over the next year, we continued to work with him. Not only would he eventually accept a halter and lead without stomping all over us, but he would also accept a blanket and saddle on his back. Because he did not like the noise of electric clippers, we didn't clip his mane. By October, as a two-year-old, he needed a trainer. We delivered him to a friend for two weeks of education.

"Jock will never make a riding mule," Rick told us after his first three days with him. "He just stands there." However, by the end of the first week, Rick sang a different tune: "I over and undered him for three hours. Then he moved and kept moving, and he's smooth. Guess he finally figured out what I wanted." [Overed and undered means using the reins to swat the animal on the rump and belly.]

Jock turned three in April 2000. He stood just shy of fifteen hands, and with his mane now clipped—I used scissors—his ears reached for the sky. His red sorrel coat shone in the sun as he led the herd in to meet us.

With strong sturdy legs beating a tattoo, he loped up the trail and stopped in a dust cloud at the corral.

It was time for grain, fresh water, and attention. When I was not looking, he grabbed the straw hat off my head or sneaked a brush from the grooming caddy. He propped his head on my shoulder, requesting an ear rub. This bargain colt now shook hands, stood to have his tail scratched, and accepted a saddle and rider. He was priceless.

A Summing Up

At this time in my life, I spent more time with animals than with people. I still had my position at Harper School, but I did most of the work on a computer at home. As time passed, I fell out of the loop with school. Teachers changed and new students came and others left. Only the animals remained constant.

After moving to the larger home along the Harper/Westfall highway, Pat and I undertook the remodeling of the house. The original home, built in the 1920s, was small. Added to it, was a larger house salvaged from the railroad depot. When these two were connected in 1985, a large living room was added giving the house a pleasing L-shaped appearance.

We began with the original structure, beginning with the floor. All the silt from a flood was removed and new floor joists and flooring installed. We gutted the old kitchen and bedroom to form one room for my study. With vinyl floor covering in the study, indoor/outdoor carpet in the dining area, sheetrock, fresh paint, new light fixtures, and the addition of a gas stove, we made a cozy place to spend cool evenings. After the new paint dried, we turned to the rest of the house. By the time that Pat's health failed, we had redone the main bedroom and added a master bath. The kitchen and utility still needed work, but we lived comfortably.

By 2000, Deidre and Dennis had purchased a home in northeast Salem, not far from where he worked for Aggregate Machinery, Inc. (AMI). Their first daughter, Kerridwen Elizabeth was born January 11, 2000. I drove down to be with Deidre and was allowed in the birthing suite during delivery. Her experience differed so much from mine. She had Dennis at her side as coach, the room was pleasant, and the atmosphere upbeat. I had watched when Cindy foaled or when kittens were born, but I had never seen a baby push into the world. It was a moment to cherish. My baby now had a baby of her own. I delighted in the feel of the infant in my arms when I rocked her at two in the morning.

Two years later in August of 2002, a second girl made her way into the world. Caitlin Alexandra was born August 5, 2002. Again I went to Salem, but this time to care for Kerridwen while Deidre was in the hospital. My heart was divided on this visit. I wanted to be present for Deidre and Kerridwen, but Pat was recovering from a strep infection that had settled in the knee that had been replaced two years previously. I needed to be with him.

The infection became a major turning point for Pat. He had undergone two other major surgeries, and with each one lost a bit of himself. He continued to drive his body to do what he wanted to do—out on the tractor, standing at his lathe, or doing any one of the million things a man can find to do. By the time that osteoporosis became an issue in his back, we had installed an underground sprinkler system in the pasture, enlarged the shop, added a barn with hayshed, and built a stout pole corral where we could work the animals.

In 2006 Pat bought a three-year-old filly—again untrained. Toughie was a sorrel that glowed red in the sunlight and flaunted a thick mane and tail of long dark red hair. After having her trained, and me taking riding lessons, I worked her at home until cold weather shut us down for that year. The next year, I fell off the haystack, tearing my left knee. That ended riding for me.

Pat added one more mule to the herd, a long yearling colt that we named Spunky. He was wild, but in the eighteen months that I had to work with him, he gentled, picked up his feet when asked, and followed me. He wouldn't lead for me, but he would stay at my heels, especially if I had alfalfa cubes in my pocket.

Each year Dennis would drive the family to Harper to see me. I sewed little dresses for the girls and made them each a muslin doll, and I watched them sprout like well-fertilized plants. I looked forward to these visits in the summer or at Thanksgiving. As for being a grandmother, I found that difficult. I saw the girls so seldom that I never really knew them. I enjoyed their excursions into the corn patch or among the flowers in my yard. They helped me with the water hose and scurried everywhere, knowing they were safe in my yard. It is only since I moved to Salem that I have built a relationship with them. After all Grandma Carol can help them with their English work, or go shopping with them for something new.

My mother died February 18, 2010 following a fall and infection. Gary could no longer care for her and had placed her in a foster home with a woman she liked. When her doctor phoned to tell me that she was in a coma, he let me know that Mother was not alone. In fact, she died with Gary by her side and Sandra on the phone telling her to let go. Because of Pat's frail health, I did not attend the graveside memorial service. Gary had already scattered her ashes somewhere in the mountains as she had requested. She and I had not been close for at least twenty years, and her death changed nothing for me.

Georgia flew in from Texas and could not understand my absence, but she did not take the time to stop and see me on her return drive from Union to Boise to catch her plane home. This was just one more lack of understanding between sisters who no longer knew each other.

Pat never understood that his spine had weakened. In an X-ray, his backbone looked like lace. It took only turning the wrong way while holding a bag of grass clippings, or cranking down on a lathe chuck to cause a compression fracture. By April of 2010 he had suffered six such fractures. He was bedfast for recovery with the last one, and never again moved freely.

Marian came to stay with me in June of 2010, as moral support while I cared for Pat. He continued to fail. Not only did he suffer from the fractures, his heart was worn out. In 1995 his doctor gave him five years. When he quit his fifty-two year habit of two packs of cigarettes a day, he added more time. Now, time was running out. By December of 2010, he spent most of his time in bed, had dropped from 165 pounds to 125, and was no longer the same man.

The end came when he decided Marian had to leave. When I tried to explain that I needed her, he said that he would hire help for me. He did not understand that it was not help with work that I needed. I told him I could not continue to care for him without her, so he told me to leave with her, not believing that I would go. I did.

Dennis and Deidre found a home for me in Salem, two blocks from where they live. Trusting them and their realtor, I bought the house unseen, and two weeks from when he told us to leave, we left Harper. Pat died in March of the following year just before his seventy-ninth birthday.

Had I not left at that time, I would be stuck with a place and animals and unable to care for all of it. God works in mysterious ways. Once I decided, all the details fell into place. Snow lay on the ground in

Harper and covered the mountains between there and Salem, but on December 17 when we left, weather was clear. A break in the storm systems lasted long enough for Marian and me to make the trip.

We began with an empty house, newly refinished but empty of furnishings. Lowe's delivered a refrigerator on the weekend, and we went shopping for beds the next week. A piece at a time, I built a new nest, one that reflects me.

Marian shouldered much of the household care for the first year while I found my way back from the edge of fatigue. In 2012 she was diagnosed as bipolar and with uterine cancer. This was a difficult period as she went through surgery, healed, and tried to find a balance with medication. Our friendship did not survive the stress, and she moved early in November of 2012.

Again, I faced a period of recuperation, this time from a mini-stroke that struck my right side that December. It left my right leg weakened, although I notice it only when I overdo. By June of 2013, I began to think about getting out, doing things, and adopting a kitty. On June 1, I brought Twiggy home. Until I had her in my lap, I did not realize just how much I had missed my kitty companions. A dark tabby with white bib and paws, she reminds me much of the Tiger I had in Klamath Falls.

With care, regular yoga sessions, and good therapists, I regained my health and my sense of self. I joined a Tai

Chi class and a writing group. In one of the most recent meetings, I experienced a break through. Out of that came the next piece of writing.

Donovan's Gift

When Donovan walked into the room last Wednesday, February 19, 2014, he brought a cloud of sadness. I did not know why until his friend Ruth read his selection about the death of his mother. The room pulsed with his feelings, and I recalled my losses—son, father, mother, partner. The cloud went home with me, stayed with me as I wrote, as I cried.

Yet, this was not about me. Once I figured out that I was carrying Donovan's grief, I could let it go. Donovan woke the empathy within me that has lain dormant because I buried it deep inside, protecting myself from hurt. With this re-awakening, came a further opening of my heart. My feelings coursed through the ether to touch another's heart.

Peter phoned the next morning to ask, "Are you okay? Do you want me to come?" He lives north of Detroit, Michigan and a trip here seemed so extravagant, especially when he had already planned to fly west in September. I told him that I would love to see him, but considering everything, he must make the decision. He did. He said, "I'm coming." He'll arrive in Portland

Thursday afternoon, February 27, rent a car, and drive down.

I first met Peter in 1960 when I was eighteen, and he was working for the Federal Aviation Administration (FAA) on the same job where my husband was a carpenter. When he returned to the east, we kept in touch, as friends do, with Christmas cards. Years later, with the coming of computers and email, we maintained a correspondence. We shared the birth of children, and the death of one. We shared problems, divorces, new relationships, anything and everything. Then, he brought his youngest son Dominic on a trip to the west about ten years ago. He stopped for a few hours with Pat and me before continuing on his way.

This is Donovan's Gift: Peter is back in my life in a whole new way.

Backbone

When all the fluff of life
Is pared away, and
I'm stripped down
To stark, skeletal bones
Of emotional pain,
An inner core remains:

Truth is important.
To be myself,
To know myself,
To accept my limits,
To acknowledge my needs,
To garner my strengths—
These make the steel
Of my will, of my life.
These are the backbone,
Boundaries of being.